Best of Make it with

PAPER

First published in the United States of America by:
Quarry Books, an imprint of
Rockport Publishers, Inc.
33 Commercial Street
Gloucester, Massachusetts 01930-5089
Telephone: (508) 282-9590
Fax: (508) 283-2742

ISBN 1-56496-428-0

10 9 8 7 6 5 4 3 2 1

Book Design
Kristen Webster
Blue Sky Limited

Cover Design
Laura Herrmann Design

Photography
Michael Lafferty

Printed in Hong Kong

Best of Make it with

PAPER

Michael J. LaFosse
and Paul Jackson

QUARRY BOOKS
Gloucester, Massachusetts

Contents

Introduction

The projects in this book were designed to be fun and simple to make. Easy to construct from almost any type of paper, these projects provide a versatile platform for creative invention. The designs and presentation ideas range from the classic to the unusual and offer something to suit every occasion. Our methods will allow you to produce winning results from even the most ordinary papers.

The paper animals presented in this book were chosen carefully, with an eye toward offering projects with a range of construction techniques. Each animal is built with a unique folding method, and each method has its own particular strengths.

Many basic box shapes have been addressed in this volume: cube, rectangle, hexagon, and heart. The folded double-wall construction provides added support to the box walls, as well as a neat, finished rim. Each of the box-lid patterns has a reinforced rim and our unique applique slot system, which allow for the insertion of an infinite variety of decorative paper elements to customize your own creations.

Flowers and butterflies are splendid subjects to render in paper and their forms are open to wide interpretation. Adapt these flower designs to create dozens of other plants and butterflies of your own.

These projects are super simple to make and a lot of fun, too! You will enjoy experimenting with the possibilities provided by different papers and after a time you may go beyond the scope of this book and apply these techniques to create dozens of other paper projects of your own, whether as gifts or for use around the home or office.

Enjoy!
Michael G. LaFosse
Author/Designer of Paper Flowers,
Paper Boxes, and Paper Animals
projects

What is a pop-up? The best answer is that pop-ups are absolutely the finest greeting cards you can send or receive! They are ingenious and fun, a wonderful mixture of magic and geometry that never fails to bring a smile when an unfamiliar design is opened for the first time. A pop-up is more than just a card; it is an object to be displayed and admired long after other cards have been put away.

The technical definition of just what is and is not a pop-up differs among designers. For me, it is a three-dimensional structure that automatically erects itself from within when unfolded. Some designers include two-dimensional effects such as rotating disks, dissolving scenes, or pull-tab movements in this definition, but for me, they lack the magic of a true pop-up and are not included in this book.

The construction of pop-up books and greeting cards began in London during the 1850s, but the geometric principles behind them go much farther back. Selferecting structures have been used for centuries by people as diverse as stage illusionists, cabinet makers, and origami designers, and since the beginning of time by Mother Nature—just watch how a flower opens. In recent years, pop-up books have become ever-more spectacular as designers try to outdo their rivals to achieve greater sales. Some of the results are truly amazing!

And yet, pop-up techniques are essentially simple. This book introduces the most versatile techniques with a number of basic—but interesting—projects. You are also encouraged to change or adapt the projects to your own specifications, rather than just copy the instructions.

But before starting a pop-up, I recommend you read *How to Use This Book*, the *Glossary & Key*, and the *Basics* section. They give invaluable advice to guide you smoothly through the design, decoration, and construction of the pop-up. Most importantly, remember that pop-ups must be made with precision, and that precision comes from thinking clearly, working patiently, and taking pride in what you make. Adopt this positive approach, and your diligence will be hugely rewarded! I have had great fun designing the pop-ups in this book and truly hope that you will have as good a time making them.

Paul Jackson
Author/Designer of Paper
Pop-Ups projects

How to Use This Book

E ach paper project begins with a list of materials and a picture of the finished product. The papers provided are marked with folding lines for your first attempts, and the templates in the back of the book can be traced to make an endless supply of patterns. To get the best possible results, the three most important things to keep in mind are: cut slowly and carefully, fold precisely, and get to know the key. The key on pages 9-11 explains the fold lines and arrows (known as the Yoshizawa/Randlet standardized origami system) that accompany each drawing in this book. If you are already familiar with this system of folding notation you will feel right at home; otherwise, spend a few moments learning to recognize these symbols and to understand the terminology.

Begin by cutting out all paper elements for the desired project from the supply sheets provided at the back of the book. You may want to photocopy both the pattern sheets and the templates, so that you will have extras for practice or in case of a mistake. Protect your work surface by placing a piece of cardboard under anything you are cutting with a blade. For most projects in this book you will find that using a tool (such as a letter opener) and a straightedge (such as a ruler) to score the fold lines on the paper elements will make folding much easier and more accurate.

Study the step-by-step photos carefully, to visually check your work. It is often helpful to look ahead at the next diagram or photo to see the results of a fold in advance. Take time to perform the folds neatly and accurately.

Though adhesives are not always necessary, you may wish to make your creations last longer by adding a little white glue or paste at key contact points. Apply adhesives sparingly and neatly, and have a damp cloth handy to wipe away any spills.

Each pop-up project begins with a list of materials and pictures of the finished pop-up. The paper elements at the back of the book are marked with folding lines for your first attempts, and the templates can be traced to make an endless supply of pop-up patterns. Use a photocopier to enlarge the templates to any size you want. To get the best possible results, the three most important things to keep in mind are: cut slowly and carefully, fold precisely, and get to know the Key. The *Glossary & Key* explains the fold lines that appear on each paper element and template at the end of this book.

Begin by cutting out all paper elements for the desired project from the supply sheets provided at the back of the book. You may want to photocopy both the paper elements and the templates, so that you will have extras for practice or in case of a mistake. Study the step-by-step photos carefully, to visually check your work. It is often helpful to look ahead at the next photo to see the results of a fold in advance. Take time to perform the folds neatly and accurately.

Glossary & Key

Because the illustrations can show only a segment of a project's folding procedure, it is helpful to know whether the paper is being folded in front or from behind. The origami system of Valley-folds and Mountain-folds uses two kinds of broken lines (see key diagram) to show when to fold toward the project's surface (valley-fold) and when to fold behind the surface (mountain-fold.)

Valley-fold - Relative to the displayed view of the paper being folded, a valley-fold is always folded in front of the project's surface. If you were to unfold a valley-fold you would see a valley-crease, which dents into the paper's surface forming a valley.

Mountain-fold - Relative to the displayed view of the paper being folded, a mountain-fold is always folded behind the project's surface. If you were to unfold a mountain-fold you would see a mountain-crease, which rises up from the paper's surface forming a mountain ridge.

Various types of arrows help make the folding instructions even clearer. These arrows are easy to understand with a quick study of the illustrated key. Whenever you see the repeat arrow in a diagram, you must apply the demonstrated folding procedure to all indicated parts of the project.

Gutter crease—This is a valley-fold in the backing sheet that supports the pop-up.

Backing sheet—The mat board that makes the stiff backing for the pop-up.

Covering layer—The paper that covers the mat board.

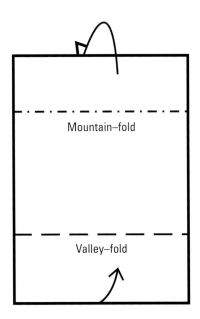

Mountain–fold

Valley–fold

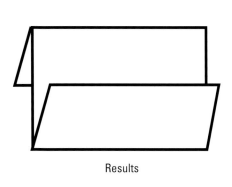

Results

Standard Symbols

Valley-fold

Mountain-fold

Directional Arrows   In Front   Behind

Turn Model Over

Insert/Apply Pressure

Repeat

Enlarged View

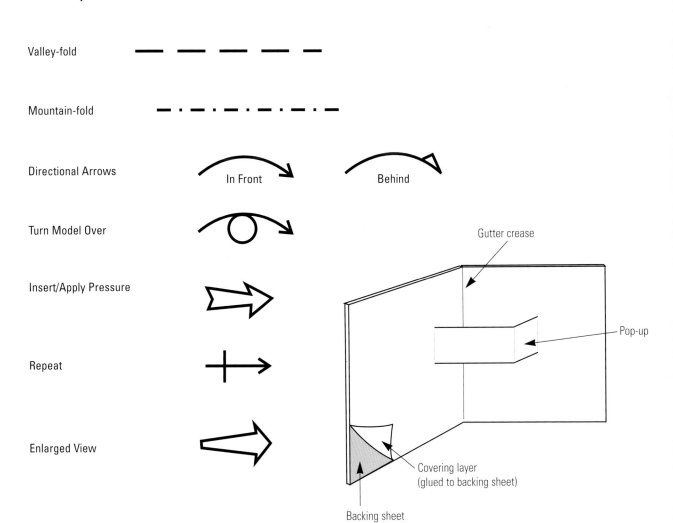

Gutter crease

Pop-up

Covering layer
(glued to backing sheet)

Backing sheet

Basics

Papers and Cardboards

The range of papers and cardboards available to you depends on two factors: where you live, and how much time and energy you are prepared to invest. Cities, larger towns, and shopping centers have art, craft, and office supply stores, which usually stock a wide range of quality papers and cardboards in attractive colors. The choice will be more limited at smaller stores away from major centers, but this selection will be wholly adequate for most paper projects. In truth, being able to find only a very limited range of basic white paper and cardboard is sufficient, particularly if you are prepared to decorate it to add color and texture (see *Decorating Paper Ideas*).

With a little more time and effort, a wider range of papers and cardboards can be obtained from other sources. Many wholesale paper suppliers sell (or even give away!) sample pads of papers and cardboards from their range, which are extremely useful if you are reluctant to buy a large sheet from a store, only to use a small piece of it.

Small printers frequently have scraps or larger sheets of paper that they will sell to you at a very low cost. If you are unable to purchase papers and cardboards, consider recycling. Use old cereal boxes, record album covers, chocolate boxes, wrapping paper, junk mail, magazine pages, scrap photocopies, old computer printouts, typing paper, and so on. The list is endless. These seemingly unlikely materials are a wonderful, virtually free source of colorful images and textures to make inspiring pop-ups.

An important consideration when selecting a paper or cardboard is its weight especially on pop-up projects. The backing sheet (see *How to Make a Backing Sheet*) needs to be stiff; otherwise it will not open completely flat. The pop-up that collapses inside it when the backing sheet is closed shut needs to be made from paper or cardboard strong enough to support itself without flopping when the design is opened, but not so thick that it prevents the backing sheet from closing around it. That said, precise weights are unimportant. All that needs to be remembered is that the medium weight paper, thick paper, or thin cardboard used to make the pop-up must be thinner than the cardboard used to make the backing sheet.

Never store paper or cardboard in a roll. The longer it is kept rolled up, the more difficult it will be to flatten. Instead, lay it flat in a safe place under a bed, between sheets of thick cardboard, in an artist's portfolio, or in a large drawer. Larger sheets can be cut into more manageable sizes for easy storage.

Equipment

In the arts and crafts field, a degree of snobbishness often exists among experienced practitioners regarding the best equipment to use. When making these paper projects, however, most of the equipment can be obtained inexpensively from a local stationery store. There is no mythology about who manufactures the sharpest utility knife or the most efficient erasers. The rule is simple: Buy the best that you can afford. Even the cheapest equipment will suffice, though you will enjoy using the equipment more if it is of better quality.

The one specialty item recommended is the selfhealing cutting mat. These magical mats heal any cut made by a blade, so that the surface never becomes rutted, as wood or thick cardboard would. For the craftsperson who works with a blade, such mats are indispensable; treated well, they will last for many years. Adhesives are unneccessary in many of the included designs, but when needed, apply them carefully and in small amounts, and use a damp cloth to clean up any excess glue.

The only other item of equipment worth mentioning separately is the cutting blade. It is inadvisable to purchase the cheapest types of retractable, snap-off blade knives. They are not very sturdy and not totally safe when cutting heavier cardboards. If you wish to purchase such a knife, buy a sturdy model that securely locks the retractable blade into cutting position. A better buy is an X-Acto-type knife with blades that can be replaced. The blades usually are sharper and make more precise cuts.

Make a Rough, Then Make It Right

The paper projects in this book are geometric structures that must be designed and assembled with precision. Because of this, you are strongly advised to make a *rough*, or a trial version, before attempting to make a finished design. Not only will the rough teach you a method for designing and assembling the project, but it will also make you aware of how you can successfully deviate from the instructions in the book to make something more personal to you than what is shown.

You may be tempted to skip the rough stage and make a finished project from scratch, but this will probably end in frustration, wasting both time and materials. Use scrap materials to construct the rough, or better still, use the same papers and cardboards as the finished design will be made from so that you can check that all is well with your choice. Making a rough will also give you the opportunity to test any decorative ideas that you may have: Will that green colored pencil stand out on the orange paper? Is the decorative border too dominant? What kind of calligraphic flourish looks best on the backing sheet?

All the necessary tests can be done at this stage: cutting out the shapes, taping on new pieces, testing decorative ideas, and generally making as much of a mess as you wish. No one will see it! In truth, these roughs can sometimes look better than the finished card if it is designed and decorated in an overly cautious way, so try to transfer some of the energy of the rough into the final version

How to Make Box Lids

Making the lid is the trickiest part of making a paper box. Although each of the featured boxes has a different shape, the six step technique outlined below can be applied to any of the box lids in the book. Once you have mastered the basic rules for constructing a lid, you will easily be able to follow the more detailed instructions that accompany each project. Have fun!

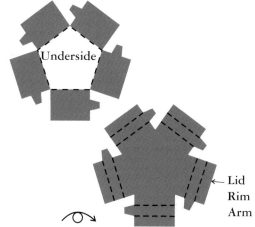

1 Valley-fold on the dashed lines of the underside of the lid paper cutout. Turn the paper over.

2 Valley-fold along the dashed lines. Each rectangular extension is referred to as a lid-rim arm.

3 (Side view of one lid-rim arm) Valley-fold the outermost segment of the lid-rim arm against the middle segment.

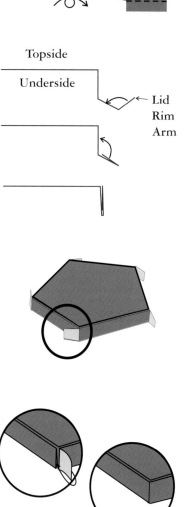

4 Valley-fold this double layer of paper against the innermost segment of the lid-rim arm. Set this three-layer lid rim at right angles to the top of the lid.

5 Apply paste to the outside of the exposed tabs. Tuck each pasted tab into its adjacent open lid-wall edge. Press firmly to seal. Allow the lid to dry on the box base.

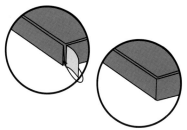

How To Make a Crease

There are three basic ways to make a crease: by hand, by scoring, or by indenting. Whichever method you choose will depend on the thickness of the paper or cardboard to be folded, and whether you are making a rough or a finished version. Everyone folds paper by hand, even if it is just to fold a letter in half, but if you are unfamiliar with scoring and indenting, it is wise to practice.

By Hand

This method is possible only with thin or medium weight paper. It is generally very inaccurate and is recommended only for roughs, when speed is important and finesse is not!

1 Before folding, draw the folds on the paper.

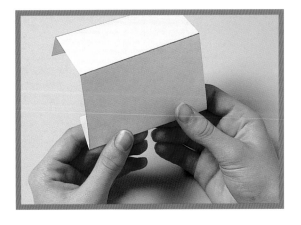

2 Make each crease as a mountain-fold. Fold carefully along the drawn line.

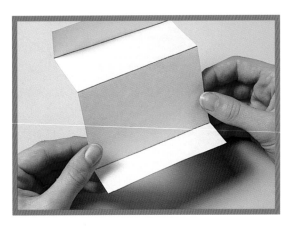

3 Some of the mountain-folds may now need to be folded back on themselves to become valleys.

Scoring

Scoring is the best-known method for creasing thick paper and cardboard, but it is not entirely recommended. The fold is made by cutting through part of the thickness of the material, thus seriously weakening it. Nevertheless, scoring is useful when making roughs.

1 With a sharp blade and a steel rule, cut through about half the thickness of the paper of cardboard along the length of the fold on the mountain side.

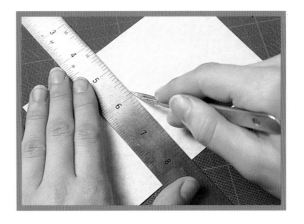

2 Bend the card backwards to make the fold. Use care; if the cut is not made to exactly the right depth, the fold will be either too stiff or too floppy.

Indenting

Indenting is the best method for folding paper or cardboard of any thickness (except for mat board, which needs to be cut). The surface of the material is not cut, but compressed, thus preserving the full strength of the material along the fold.

1 Turn a blade upside down, so that the blunt tip of the back of the blade is in contact with the paper or cardboard, then compress the material along the fold. Do not break the surface. Do this on the valley side the crease.

2 Bend the card forward to make the fold (the opposite way from when scoring). Compared to the scoring technique, the fold is much stronger.

How to Make a Backing Sheet

It is essential that the backing sheet on any pop-up is stiff, otherwise the pop-up structure will not fully open when the backing sheet is unfolded. To achieve this, the backing sheet is usually made from mat board, though sometimes a design will be strong enough if the backing sheet is made from thinner cardboard or thick paper.

Here then is the method for making a backing sheet from mat board.

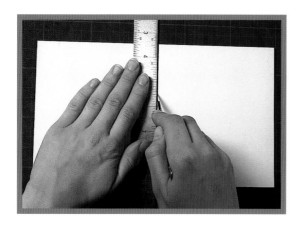

1 Cut out a piece of mat board to the size of the finished pop-up when it is opened flat. Draw a line down the center. Cut the card in two down the center line. Accuracy is important.

2 Lay one half over the other and trim off any excess to ensure that they are identical.

3 Butt the two halves up against each other and tape them together.

4 Turn the mat board over and neatly trim off the excess tape at both ends.

5 Turn over again. This is the basic backing sheet. However, it needs covering with a layer of medium weight paper to hide the tape and to coordinate the color of the backing sheet with the pop-up on top of it.

6 In a well-ventilated room or outdoors, spray adhesive on the backing sheet. Glue from a tube may also be used, but the spray is quicker and better.

7 Turn the glued backing sheet upside down and lower it onto the back of the covering layer of medium weight paper.

8 Trim off excess covering layer paper by carefully cutting around the edge of the mat board.

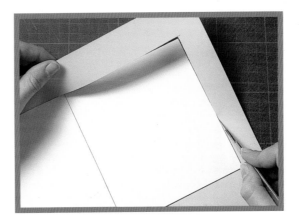

9 Turn over. Fold the backing sheet and covering layer in half and press firmly to make a sharp gutter crease down the center. This completes the backing sheet.

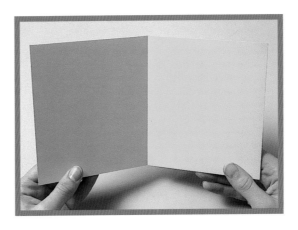

Painting and Decorating

Whether you choose plain or patterned paper, the shapes in these projects are distinct enough to stand on their own. If you would like to decorate the projects to make them more realistic or more fanciful, you can use acrylic paint, inks, markers, crayons, stencils, appliqués, and even monoprinting. A few favorite decorating techniques are illustrated here, use them as inspiration to create beautiful designs of your own.

Add Shine

Apply a rainbow of shimmering luster with iridescent acrylic paint. These paints come in many colors, and are permanent and fade-resistant. For best results, paint a dark base-coat first. Paint on a smooth, seamless field of iridescence, or try using brushes, rollers, sponges, or rags to make textured and mottled effects.

Sponge Paint

Daubing on paint makes it easy to produce textures and multicolored effects. Use a sponge or wadded rag to dab or streak broken areas of color over the paper. Use a separate sponge or rag for each color and apply dark colors first. Experiment with smudging or scraping the applied paints while they are wet. Acrylic tube colors are the best choice for this technique, since they are flexible and water resistant when dry. Use only non-toxic colors around children.

Add Texture

You can copy the texture of many different surfaces with the crayon rubbing technique. Place paper over the chosen texture and rub with a crayon. Oil pastels, colored pencils, and varying the amount of pressure and shape of stroke will produce different effects.

Japanese Style

What better way to ornament koi than with a Japanese painting style, brush (fude), and ink (sumi). To get this effect, paint on heavyweight, bright white, absorbent paper. Black, crimson and vermilion inks are best for koi. Prepare a liquid painting solution, load the brush with ink or paint, and touch the tip to the surface of the paper. Allow the ink or paint to bleed into the paper as you go: aim for rounded shapes with slightly soft edges. You may want to practice on ordinary newsprint first.

Appliqués

Appliqués decorate paper with very precise, rich patterns. Here, colored shapes for a parrot are cut out, then pasted in place. This can be done before or after cutting out the final paper form. Draw a light pencil line to indicate the proper placement of the various elements.

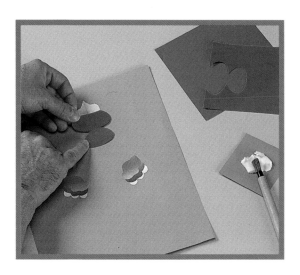

Monoprints

1 Monoprinting can generate a wide variety of effects on paper. The basic materials needed are substrate, paint, paper and a burnishing tool. Many types of surfaces and paints will work to create monoprints: here, we used a stiff plastic board and acrylic tube paints. To get this effect, apply color in parallel rows directly from the tube and smear with a piece of cardboard.

2 Place substrate-coated paper face-down on the cardboard and rub with the back of a spoon to impress the paint on the surface of the paper.

3 Peel the paper up and let dry. It is possible to obtain several prints from one prepared surface.

Stencils

1 Stencils will also produce rich patterns and textures on paper. You can color or paint stencils by hand, or use spray paint for a fast finish. To stencil with spray paint, sandwich the chosen paper between the stencil and an "overspray" sheet. The overspray sheet will protect your work area. Make sure that the stencil lies completely flat against the surface of the paper to be decorated. Spray paint in an even, controlled manner—or experiment by spraying short bursts, long and narrow bands, circular patterns, etc.

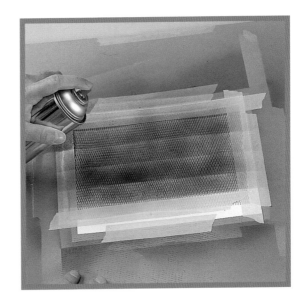

2 Each method will yield different results from the same stencil. Carefully remove the stencil and paper from the overspray sheet and allow to dry. Always work in well-ventilated areas and use a respirator if suggested by the manufacturer.

Cube Box

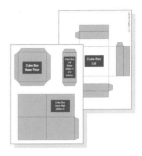

How to Build a Cube Box

These perfectly square containers combine utility with simplicity and beauty. Make several cube boxes to "nest" or stack together, or use paper in primary colors to make a set with different color tops and bottoms. If you prefer patterned to plain papers, use simple, bold designs to highlight the perfect geometry of the cube. Pair textured and glossy papers for a subtle contrast between boxes and lids of the same color. You can also weave two solid colors together to give the lid a checkerboard or triangle pattern.

Materials

- *Cube Box paper elements*
- *Scissors and/or X-Acto knife*
- *Paste or glue stick*
- *Brush for applying paste*

Cube Box Tips

- *Use a straightedge and a razor knife to cut neat edges for the decorative lid elements.*
- *It is not necessary to glue the ornamental lid elements into the top of the lid. This will enable you to switch the patterns whenever you wish.*
- *Allow extra distance between the inside of the fold lines of the decorative lid elements if you make boxes from heavier paper.*
- *To make a nesting set, photocopy the pattern on a copier with a zoom function. Reduce or enlarge by 15% for a perfect fit.*

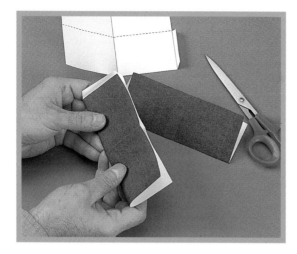

1 Valley-fold the short lines of the base wall; then carefully align the opposing long edges and fold in half so that the colored side of the paper shows. Repeat with the other base wall element. Make the folded edges sharp and clean by running the side of your thumbnail along the folded paper.

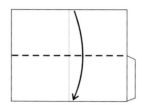 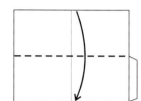

2 Apply paste to the outside of one of the tabs. The outside of a tab is on the same side as the colored side of the paper. Connect the two base wall elements together, end to end, by inserting the pasted tab of one between the folded layers of the other. The pasted tab should stick to only one inside surface of the base wall element.

Apply Paste

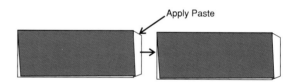

3 Apply paste to the outside of the exposed tab and bring the two ends of the base wall element together. Tuck the pasted tab between the folded layers of the end of the paper and press firmly to make a good fit.

4 Make the cube even by adjusting the creases. This is the base wall of the box: The top edge is folded; the bottom is an open, double edge of paper. The tabs of the floor will be pasted between the open edges of paper.

Fold the tabs of the box floor, as shown, apply paste, and carefully insert into the base wall.

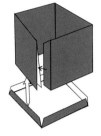 

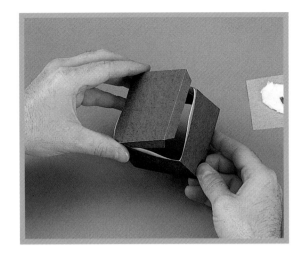

5 Carefully fold the edges of the lid. Begin with the underside and valley-fold the innermost creases. Unfold and turn the paper over. Make the valley-folds indicated and crease them to close at right angles to the top of the lid. Apply paste to one or both sides of each tab.

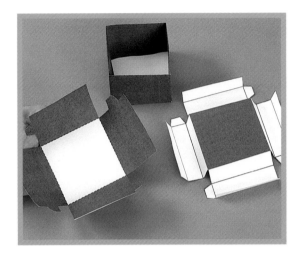

6 Tuck each pasted tab into its adjacent open lid-wall edge. Press firmly to seal. Allow the lid to dry on the box base.

7 Fold the tab edge on each of the lid elements. Make this fold very sharp and clean. Weave the four elements, alternating the colors, and fold tab edges at right-angles to the finished checkerboard top.

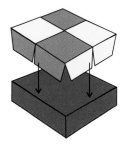

8 Insert tab edge (with or without paste at first) into the open edges of the perimeter of the box lid.

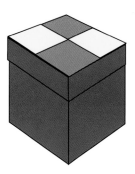

9 The finished puzzle box. You may further divide the colored strips and re-weave for smaller and more numerous checks.

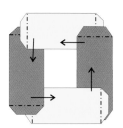

Cube Box Gallery

These checkerboards are created by cutting narrower strips and basket-weaving the top of the lid. Be sure to make strips that are even and clean-cut.

Each of these colorful nesting boxes is fifteen percent smaller than the size before it. Use the zoom function of a photocopy machine to reduce or enlarge the pattern for different sizes.

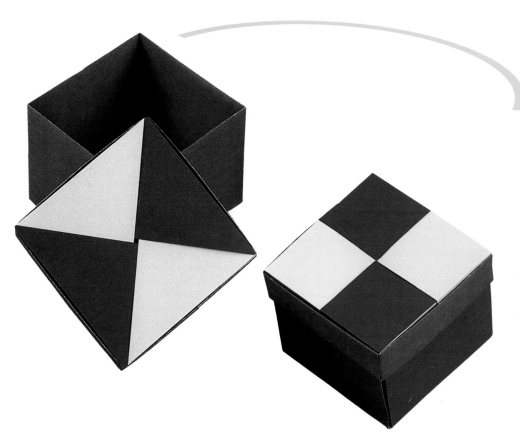

Simple, bold patterns are very effective for this project. The woven triangle pattern was created by cutting out four triangle-shaped elements, with tabs. Each triangle is the size of one-quarter of the lid, when a line is drawn diagonally from one corner to an opposite corner.

Frame Box

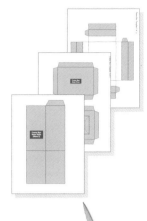

How to Build a Frame Box

This box is the perfect container for treasures, keepsakes, or souvenirs. A cut-out in the lid lets you frame photographs, or scrapbook items such as invitations, theater tickets, newspaper clippings, wedding or birth announcements, or any other mementos you hold dear. Frame a baby picture and keep a lock of hair or first tooth in the box. Send a gardener friend a box of seeds with the seed packet framed on the lid. The frame box is wonderfully adaptable for all sorts of little gifts and special occasions.

Frame Box Tips

- *This is a good box to make from heavier materials such as textured, cover-weight papers. Use a ruler and letter opener or similar tools to pre-score such materials to make folding easier.*
- *If you pre-score the folding edges of the inside of the frame opening, you will get neater and more accurate results.*
- *Allow a little more distance between the inside of the fold lines of the frame if you make boxes from heavier paper.*
- *You should glue the frame elements to the top of the lid, but it is not necessary to apply glue to items under the frame.*

Materials

- *Frame Box paper elements*
- *Scissors and/or X-Acto knife*
- *Paste or glue stick*
- *Brush for applying paste*
- *Ruler or other straightedge*
- *Scoring tool (such as a letter opener)*

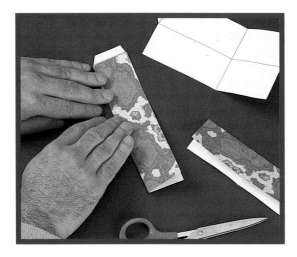

1 Valley-fold the short lines of the base wall; then carefully align the opposing long edges and fold in half so that the colored side of the paper shows. Repeat with the other base wall element. Make the folded edges sharp and clean by running the side of your thumbnail along the folded paper.

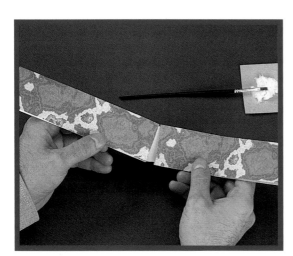

2 Apply paste to the outside of one of the tabs. The outside of a tab is on the same side as the colored side of the paper. Connect the two base wall elements together, end to end, by inserting the pasted tab of one between the folded layers of the other. The pasted tab should adhere to only one inside surface of the base wall element.

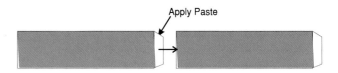

Apply Paste

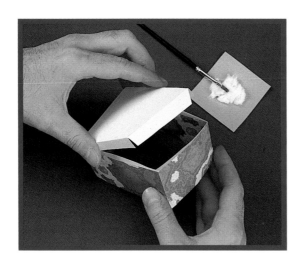

3 Apply paste to the outside of the remaining exposed tab and bring the two short ends of the base wall element together. Tuck the pasted tab between the folded layers of the end of the paper and press firmly to make a good fit. Make the rectangle even by adjusting the segment creases. You now have the base wall of the box. The top edge is folded, and the bottom of the rectangle is an open, double edge of paper. The tabs of the floor of the box will be pasted between these open edges of paper.

Prepare the floor of the box by folding the tabs to stand vertically around the edge. Apply paste to both sides of each tab. Carefully fit the tabs into the bottom, open edges of the base wall.

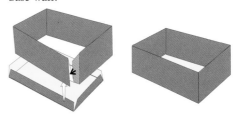

4 Fold the edges of the lid. Begin with the underside and valley-fold the innermost creases. Unfold and turn the paper over. Make the valley-folds indicated and crease them to close at right angles. Apply paste to each tab.

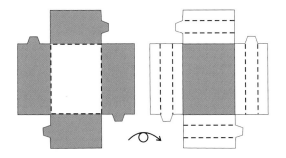

5 Tuck each pasted tab into its adjacent open lid-wall edge. Press firmly to seal. Allow lid to dry on the box base.

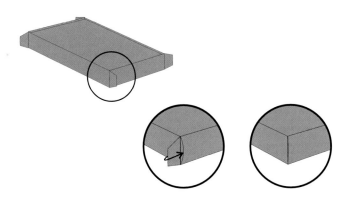

6 With an X-Acto knife, cut out the rectangular center, indicated by the innermost dotted line, then cut on the four angled, dotted lines (a). This opens the center of the frame. Valley-fold the cut edges outward and the tab edges inward (b). Turn the frame over and set the tab edges at right-angles to the face of the frame (c).

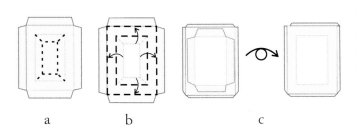

a   b   c

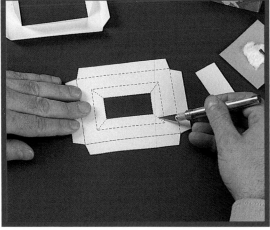

7 Insert the frame tabs into the open edges at the perimeter of the box lid. You may use glue or paste for permanence.

8 A photo or decorative paper may be placed between the lid and the frame before assembly. You may also experiment with other shapes for the cutout center of the frame element.

9 The finished frame box. This example shows off the colorful box paper.

Frame Box Gallery

A photograph inserted in this handsome box gives added meaning to a gift, especially if it reflects the contents of the box.

Any design that fits on the cube box lid can be adapted to the frame box lid. Here, we have borrowed the woven triangle pattern.

Create amusing and colorful boxes by cutting out shaped insert elements and arranging them in various ways. You can use decorative lid ideas from any of the other projects in this book.

Puzzle Box

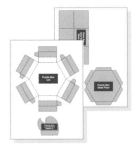

How to Build a Puzzle Box

The puzzle box adds wonderful possibilities to the art of presentation. The ornamental lid segments may be created from any paper—in one, two, three or six colors. Design your own segment shapes to create an infinite combination of lid patterns, or omit the puzzle pieces to make a distinguished hexagonal box. Attractively patterned papers are especially suitable for making the box without the puzzle lid.

It is easy to scale these boxes to any dimensions you require, due to the simple geometry involved. The pattern is adaptable to many materials other than paper. Try using colored aluminum craft foils or paper-backed fabric. The basic shape of this box makes it very versatile indeed.

Materials

- *Puzzle Box paper elements*

- *Scissors and/or X-Acto knife*

- *Paste or glue stick*

- *Brush for applying paste*

Puzzle Box Tips

- *Use sharp scissors or a pointed razor knife with a fresh blade to cut out the paper pieces. This will give you cleaner edges and a better-looking box.*

- *When removing paper pieces, cut from the back side of the paper provided. Cut just inside the outlines.*

- *Where mountain-folds are shown in the diagram steps for folding the lid, there are valley-fold dashed lines on the other side of the paper. This way, fold lines will not show on the outside of the finished model.*

- *If you make more boxes from heavier paper, pre-crease all fold lines by scoring with a straightedge and scoring tool.*

- *Ordinary white paste, or convenient glue sticks, are preferable to liquid glues for this project. Use only the smallest amount of glue, to prevent warping.*

1 Valley-fold the short lines of the base wall; then carefully align the opposing long edges and fold in half so that the colored side of the paper shows. Repeat with the other base wall element. Make the folded edges sharp and clean by running the side of your thumbnail along the folded paper.

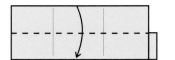 

2 Apply paste to the outside of one of the tabs. The outside of a tab is on the same side as the colored side of the paper. Connect the two base wall elements together, end to end, by inserting the pasted tab of one between the folded layers of the other. The pasted tab should stick to only one inside surface of the base wall element.

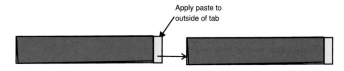

Apply paste to outside of tab

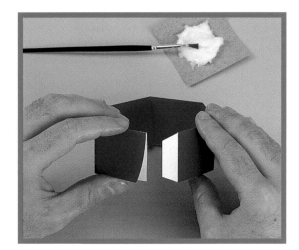

3 Apply paste to the outside of the exposed tab and bring the two ends of the base wall element together. Tuck the pasted tab between the folded layers of the end of the paper and press firmly to make a good fit.

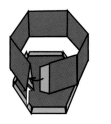

4 Sharpen and adjust the segment creases to create an evenly shaped hexagonal ring. This ring forms the walls of the base of the box. The top of the ring is a folded edge, and the bottom of the ring is an open, double edge of paper. The tabs of the floor of the box are pasted between these open edges of paper.

Prepare the floor of the box by folding the tabs to stand vertically around the hexagonal edge of the piece. Apply paste to both sides of each tab. Carefully fit the tabs into the bottom, open edges of the base wall assembly.

5 Carefully fold the edges of the lid. Begin with the underside and valley-fold the innermost creases. Unfold and turn the paper over. Make the valley-folds indicated and crease them to close at right angles to the top of the lid. You should now have a lid with a blue top and yellow sides.

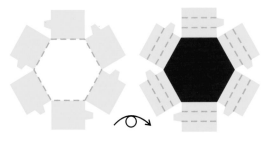

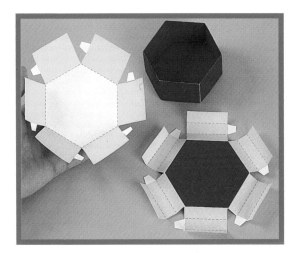

6 Apply paste to the tabs, and tuck each pasted tab into its adjacent open lid-wall edge. Press firmly to seal. Allow the lid to dry on the box base.

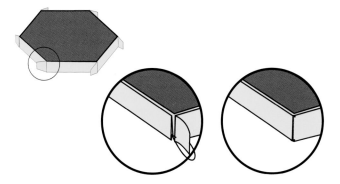

7 Fold the tab edge of each of the six puzzle elements. Make this fold very sharp and clean.

8 Insert the tab ends of the puzzle elements into the edges of the box lid. Alternate the colors and make sure that the pointed end of each shape is visible. The result will be a wonderful pattern. You can experiment with other ways to arrange the papers in the lid, or design other shapes of your own.

Apply Paste

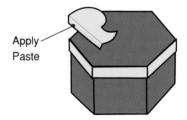

9 The finished puzzle box.

Puzzle Box Gallery

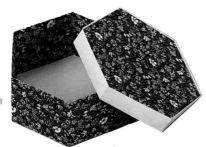

There are endless possibilities with modular lid elements. Some element shapes can be installed in more than one way. The even number of box sides allows for many color possibilities.

You can keep the construction simple by using ornate papers or get fancy by applying delicate cutout shapes to make these decorative flower themes.

Here are coordinated desktop accessories: a pencil holder and a paper clip box. The pencil holder can be weighted with uncooked rice or dried beans to prevent tipping and support pencils in the cup.

Lotus Box

How to Build a Lotus Box

The lotus symbolizes creation, and this lotus can be created anywhere there is paper. An ideal project to teach to children who can then teach their friends! This origami box requires no glue or scissors to make: It is folded from square paper. To make paper square, simply fold the short edge of any paper rectangle against the long edge, forming a triangle with a rectangular remnant along one edge. Trim away the remnant and unfold the paper. You now have a square sheet of paper. Easy to do anywhere, use lightweight paper for best results.

Lotus Box Tips

- *Be sure that the papers are cut perfectly square and to the proper size.*
- *Sharpen all creases with the side of your thumbnail to make them look neat and help them keep their shape longer.*
- *Cut up colorful old magazines for material. The weight and size of magazine paper is ideal for this project.*

Materials

- *Two sheets of eight-inch square paper, one green and one yellow*

- *One seven and one half-inch sheet of green paper*

1 The folding of the lid and the base are identical. The base paper is one-eighth smaller than the lid paper, so it will fit inside the finished lid. Begin with the largest green paper—with the white side up. (a) Valley-fold paper in half, corner to corner, both ways. Unfold the paper to see that the two fold lines will cross in the middle of the square.

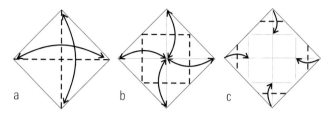

2 (b) Valley-fold the four corners to the center of the square. Unfold the paper. (c) Valley-fold the four corners of the square to the center of the fold lines created in the previous step. (d) Valley-fold the green folded edges in, along the crease lines already made. (e) The models will now look like the illustration shown. Turn the models over. (f) (magnification) Valley-fold the opposite side edges to the vertical center line of the square. Unfold.

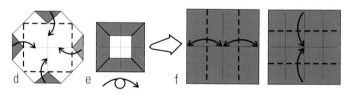

3 (g) Valley-fold the top and bottom edges to the horizontal center line. (h) Flip up the lower flap to the top of the model to reveal the white side of the paper. (i) Valley-fold the lower green corners to the square angled crease lines. (j) Return the flap to its original position. Repeat steps g, h, and i on the other side of the paper.

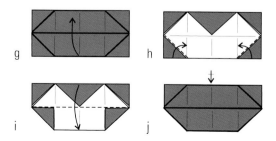

4 (k) The model should now look like this. Open the model from the center. (l) Push in the corners and square the four box walls. (m) Follow steps a-l to fold the smaller green paper (for the lid). Both the lid and the base should match the drawing and one should fit inside the other.

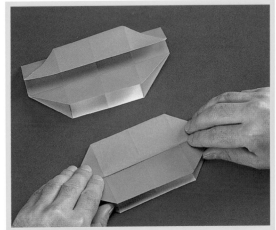

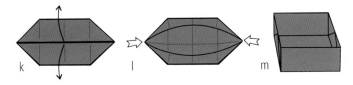

5 Use the yellow square for the lotus top. (a) Begin with the white side up. Fold the square in half, edge to edge, both ways. (b) Unfold to reveal the white paper again. (c) Fold the four corners of the square to the center of the paper. (d) Fold the four new corners to the center. The model will look like the illustration and will have two layers of four yellow "petals" on this side.

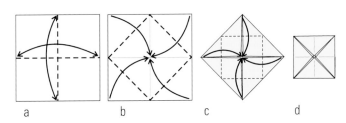

6 (e) (magnification) Fold the four petal corners of the first layer to the center of their outer edge. (f) Model will look like the illustration. (g) Fold the petal corners of the second (inner) layer to the framed corners of the model. (h) Model will look like the illustration. Turn the model over.

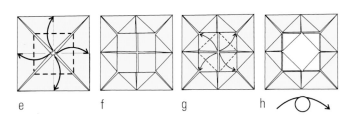

7 (i) Fold the corners of this square to the center. (j) Unfold and set at right angles to the square base. These are the base points. (k) Turn the model over. (l) Slightly elevate the eight petal points marked by dots in the drawing. This is the lotus form.

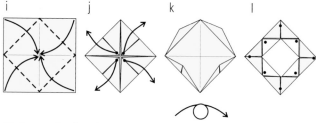

i   j   k   l

8 Insert the four base corners into the open edges of the box lid.

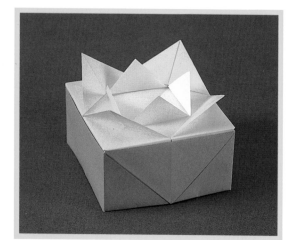

9 The finished lotus box.

Lotus Box Gallery

Fold several smaller lotus elements and insert them into the opening of the main lotus. You can experiment with colors and make more petals with a few scissor cuts.

Here the lotus box is used as a photo frame. Unfold the lotus and insert a photo or a slip of contrasting colored paper, then re-fold with the element enclosed.

Standard origami papers come in a wide variety of colors and patterns. All can be used for the lotus box.

Fan Pop-Ups

Cartoon Explosion
The Cartoon Explosion project illustrates the fan pop-up technique and the drama of its 180-degree swivel.

Vase of Flowers
In the Vase of Flowers, the pink flower actually propels the "blooming" of the yellow flower.

Fan pop-ups are among the most dramatic and humorous of all pop-ups. This is primarily because the pop-up shape swivels through 180 degrees as the card is opened, to create movement. The technique is similar to that of the silhouette pop-up, in that both techniques create a "V" shape that straddles the gutter crease. Fan pop-ups, however, are not flat across the bottom (as are silhouette pop-ups) but are shallow "V" shapes themselves. This small change of angle creates a dramatic swiveling effect, though the angles themselves need to be calculated with precision if the effect is to work well. So, although fan pop-ups are simple and quick to create, they are subtle and need careful construction.

The two projects show different effects the fan design affords: Cartoon Explosion has an energetic, jagged outline, but the pop-up mechanism still works in the conventional way. In the Vase of Flowers, notice how the folds on the pink flower provide the power for the yellow flower to open, to create an unusual off-center pop-up effect. You could try adding a third flower, or even a fourth, each one being powered by the preceding one!

Fan Pop-Up Tips

- *Compare fan pop-ups with silhouette pop-ups. The difference is in the use of angles—in particular, the angle of the "V" across the gutter and the angle across the bottom of the pop-up.*
- *To learn how changing angles can affect the swiveling of a fan pop-up, spend fifteen minutes making a series of quick studies in which the angle of the "V" across the gutter and the angle across the bottom of the pop-up change in relation to each other.*
- *Accuracy in measuring angles is key; if your protractor is old and dirty, buy a new one—they are very inexpensive. If you are unfamiliar with how to use one, practice before making a pop-up.*

Materials

*For **Cartoon Explosion**, you will need*
- *Cartoon Explosion paper elements*
- *Thin white cardboard:*
  10" x 6" (25 cm x 15 cm) and
  8" x 5" (20 cm x 13 cm)

*For **Vase of Flowers**, you will need*
- *Vase of Flowers paper elements*
- *Sturdy backing sheet (see page 16):*
  8" x 7" (20 cm x 19 cm)
- *Covering layer: medium weight, soft pink paper, 8" x 7" (20 cm x 19 cm) or larger*

Equipment

- *Craft knife*
- *Glue*
- *Marker pens*
- *Pencil and eraser*
- *Protractor*
- *Ruler*

Cartoon Explosion

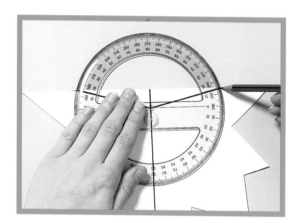

1 On the backing sheet, use a protractor to measure a very shallow "V" shape close to the top edge. The angle to each side of the gutter crease is 76 degrees. The paper elements and templates provide the correct angle for your convenience. Fold and unfold the gutter crease.

2 Glue the paper element tabs along the bottom edge of the pop-up to the line of the shallow "V." Note that the pop-up does not stand upright, but lies almost flat when the sheet is fully opened. Fold the backing sheet in half to check that the mechanism works well.

3 With a pencil, draw the explosion. For extra 3-D effect, allow "BANG!" to run from the backing sheet onto the pop-up and then right across it. Erase any unwanted lines.

4 Color in the explosion using bright marker pens—the gaudier it is, the better it will look! Use a black marker to outline some of the shapes.

Backing Sheet Shapes

This project proves that the gutter crease need not be in the middle of the backing sheet, and the backing sheet need not be rectangular—it can be any shape at all, however bizarre! Think hard about the shape of the backing sheet and where to place the gutter crease. The conventional rectangular backing sheet is often totally adequate, but to use backing sheets in a creative way can transform an ordinary design into something special. For further examples of irregular backing sheets and off-center gutter creases, look at the Locomotive, Car, and Photo Frame pop-ups.

Vase of Flowers

1 Cut out and fold the pink flower. Two mountain-folds and one valley-fold (folding from the back of the flower image) enable the flower to fold shut; if you are familiar with origami, this fold pattern will be recognized as a "waterbomb base."

2 Similarly, cut out and fold the yellow flower. If using the templates to create your own flowers, use the same medium weight, soft pink paper as on the covering layer. Collapse it shut along the folds. As with the previous flower, the angles between the folds are 45 degrees or 90 degrees. Measure them with a protractor, or if you are feeling confident, estimate them by eye.

3 Apply glue to the uncolored tab attached to the pink flower paper element. Lower the collapsed yellow flower onto the glue, such that the center point of the yellow flower touches the center fold on the pink one.

4 Now, collapse the pink flower shut, so that the other half of the glued tab sticks to the top surface of the yellow flower. Check the result against the photograph of the completed project.

5 Make a sturdy backing sheet and covering layer. Draw the artwork, leaving a space where the pop-up flowers will be attached. The design is perhaps best created even before folding the flowers, so that the pop-up flowers and the design on the covering layer are well coordinated.

6 Apply glue to the underside of the pink flower paper element, then glue it to the covering layer as shown. The center point of the flower exactly touches the gutter, leaving angles of 45 degrees above and below it, to the right-hand side of the gutter. Then, apply glue to the top surface of the flower. Fold the backing sheet shut, so that it sticks to the glued surface. Unfold to reveal the finished design.

Fan Pop-Up Gallery

Top Hat

Like the Cartoon Explosion, the opening of the design sees the pop-up hat swivel dramatically into an upright position. Notice how the artwork carefully continues from the hat onto the head, so that the complete drawing is as convincing as possible.

Locomotive

Compare this design with the Car pop-up. Technically, they look very similar. However, creating it as a fan pop-up means that the locomotive leans back a little, and is easier to see; the Car stands upright. The subtle use of angles can help create exactly the effect that you want.

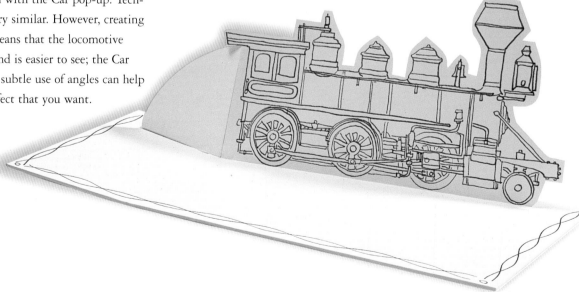

Raspberry

The dramatic swiveling of the pop-up makes the fan technique perfect for humorous designs. Here, the tongue swivels downwards as the card opens.

Bookworm

Here, two fan pop-ups have been made: one for the book, the other for the reader. Notice that the reader is flatter that the book. This serves no technical purpose, but makes the design look a little more complex, and hence more interesting.

Songbird

Here, the pop-up has been placed low down on the gutter, so that it does not protrude much above the top edge of the backing sheet. The effect creates a restrained, quiet pop-up, helped by the sensitive use of colored pencil.

Tent Pop-Ups

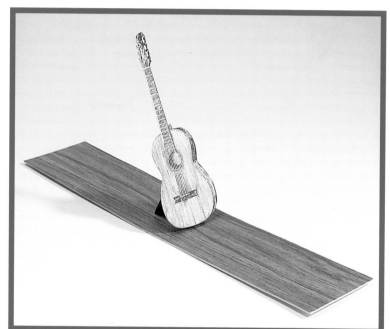

Guitar
The Guitar uses the basic tent technique.

Stars
Stars incorporates an unusual twist, with the two stars sharing a fold.

It could be said that the tent technique is the silhouette technique "turned upright." They are fundamentally similar, yet achieve different pop-up effects. The technique is also a relative of the scenery flats technique, in that both display a flat pop-up shape on the front of a supporting tab.

The guitar project shows the basic tent technique. Once learned, it can be used to display any shape with any silhouette, or even be turned sideways, as in the Balloon idea at the end of the chapter. Simple, versatile, and particularly good at displaying objects in a seemingly unsupported way, the tent technique creates a feeling of lightness that is unusual in a pop-up. In the Stars project, the ingenious way in which the two stars are joined by a fold is an unusual but effective use of tent technique. To make more stars, simply continue the joining pattern and make a longer gutter crease.

Tent Pop-Up Tips

- *The supporting tab behind the main pop-up is best made so that it slots through the covering layer. In this way, its glue tabs are hidden out of sight and the final design looks much tidier.*
- *Note how some of the projects (Stars) and gallery pop-ups (Clothesline, Eiffel Tower, Campsite, Easel) use the basic tent form as part of the final design, whereas others (Guitar, Balloon, Photo Frame) hide it behind a flat cut-out.*
- *If you are looking for an elegant technical challenge, try making the Guitar and Stars projects from a single sheet of stiff cardboard, instead of from separate pieces. The pop-up shapes are cut from the backing sheet, lifted upright along folds where folds are currently made, and glued together over the gutter.*

Materials

*For **Guitar**, you will need*
- *Guitar paper elements*
- *Sturdy backing sheet (see page 16): 14" x 3" (35 cm x 7.5 cm)*
- *Covering layer: Wood-grain shelf paper, 14" x 3" (35 cm x 7.5 cm) or larger*
- *Support: Shelf paper, 5" x 1" (12.5 cm x 2.5 cm)*

*For **Stars**, you will need*
- *Stars paper elements*
- *Sturdy backing sheet (see page 16): 11" x 6" (28 cm x 15 cm)*
- *Covering layer: Medium weight red paper, 11" x 6" (28 cm x 15 cm) or larger*

Equipment

Craft knife
Glue
Colored pencils
Pencil and eraser
Pair of compasses
Ruler
Protractor
Gold marker pen (optional)

Guitar

1 Fold the covering layer in half. Draw a line 1" (2.5 cm) long, ³/₄" (2 cm) away from the gutter crease. The length of the line will match the width of the supporting tab. Its distance from the gutter dictates how upright the tab will stand—the closer to the gutter it is, the more vertical the tab will be.

2 Cut along the drawn line through both layers. Make sure that the cut is exactly parallel to the gutter crease. Cutting through both layers at once guarantees that the construction will be symmetrical.

3 Open the covering layer. Cut out and fold the support from the guitar paper elements. Push the tabs through the slits on the covering layer and glue or tape them in place underneath.

4 Make a sturdy backing sheet. Spray the front surface with an even layer of spray adhesive.

5 With great care, lower the folded covering layer onto the backing sheet, so that the gutter crease on the covering layer is exactly on top of the crease on the backing sheet. Take as much time as you need to do this perfectly.

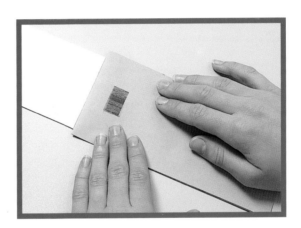

6 Close the backing sheet onto the other half of the covering layer. Open the pop-up and trim the excess covering layer paper. If the backing sheet will not open flat, this is probably because the covering layer was not positioned accurately at step 5, so reposition it—the spray adhesive allows you to do this.

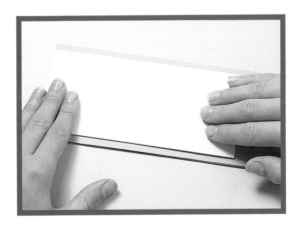

7 Cut out the guitar paper element. If you make the guitar from the template, use thin cardboard. Apply glue to the front of the supporting tab and fix the guitar to it; if the shape is particularly large or spindly, reinforce it with an extra layer of cardboard. Here, the guitar neck has an extra layer glued to it to prevent it from bending backwards over a period of time.

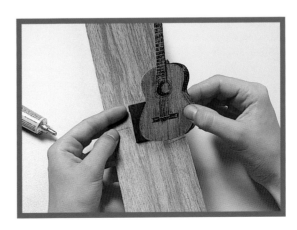

Stars

1 Cut out the Stars paper elements, or follow the templates and make your own from thin white card rather than paper (so that the stars will be sturdy).

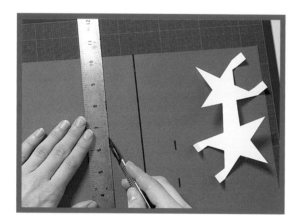

2 On a sheet of medium weight red paper, the same size or a little larger than the sturdy backing sheet, draw a central gutter crease. Then, 3" (8 cm) away from the crease on each side, draw four short lines to coincide with the position of the tabs on the stars' feet. Cut along the four lines. Note that this is the back of the sheet, so position the cuts the reverse of how they would be on the front side.

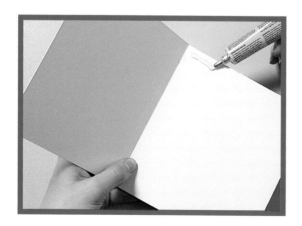

3 Make an 11" x 6" (28 cm x 15 cm) sturdy backing sheet, but do not cover the card with paper. Apply glue to the front.

4 With great care, lower the glued surface of the backing sheet onto the colored layer of paper, so that the two center creases exactly align. Take your time and do this perfectly.

5 Trim off the excess paper to create a tidy edge to the backing sheet. This can be done without a ruler: the thickness of the card will keep your knife running straight.

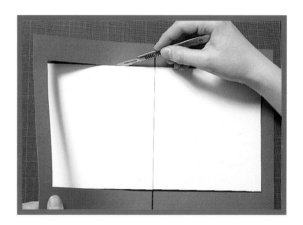

6 Carefully push the tabs on the stars into the slits made in step 2. This will be made easier if, back in step 3, glue is not applied around the tab areas. When the feet are all securely inserted, fold the whole card in half to finally create the gutter crease through the colored layer.

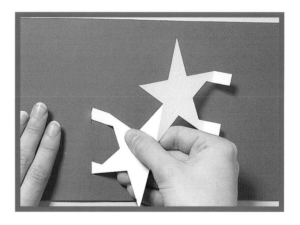

Tent Pop-Up Gallery

Balloon

The supporting tab used to support the Guitar may also be used with the backing sheet standing upright, so that a shape (here, a balloon) can apparently hang suspended in mid-air. Compare this design with the Celebration project—it is technically similar, but simpler.

Photo Frame

This is indeed an eccentric design: the pop-up is bigger than the backing sheet. Nevertheless, this simple project is a wonderful way to send an important photograph to someone, so that they may easily display it. A larger backing sheet would make the overall design look clumsy. The photograph rests on a support similar to that in the Guitar.

Eiffel Tower

This is one of the simplest pop-ups to make, yet quite dramatic. Two images of the Eiffel Tower are glued to the backing sheet astride the gutter and glued together at the top.

Campsite

The tent features a conventional support with an extra triangle glued across the middle to create the front flap of the tent. A fold down the center of the triangle allows it to collapse when the backing sheet is closed shut. The flagpole is glued to the gutter crease.

Clothesline

Cotton thread is a material that is underused in pop-ups. It has many interesting technical uses, and it creates a satisfying airiness that contrasts well with conventional solid blocks of paper or cardboard.

Coil Pop-Ups

Coil Heart

The Coil Heart project shows what can be done with a simple application of the coil technique.

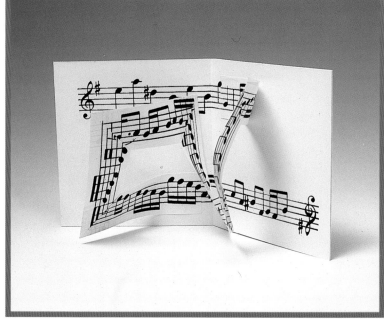

Musical Score

The Musical Score is a bit more complex.

The coil technique is a curious one: it requires little or no measuring, and no careful construction, and the final result is often apparently nongeometric, even haphazard. The result can appear so random that to the uninitiated, even the simplest coil can seem clever. The only technical subtlety is to know how many revolutions the coil should have: too few and the backing sheet will not open fully flat; too many and the coil will flop about and not stretch open. As a general rule, between two and three revolutions should be about right, depending upon whether the ends are glued to the backing sheet near to or far from the valley-fold.

The Coil Heart, a pleasingly simple and quick-to-make design, is good for beginners because the pop-up mechanism is very reliable and requires no measuring. The Musical Score differs from the other step-by-step coil designs in the chapter because the coil does not spiral inward to a point of origin, but remains a constant width, rather like a spiral staircase.

Coil Pop-Up Tips

- *Learn the basic technical difference between the flat, simple one-piece coil used to make the Coil Heart and the multiple-piece coil used to make the Musical Score. Once the difference is understood, many different pop-ups can be made.*

- *In the rough, experiment with gluing the coils to different places on the backing sheet. In some positions, the coil will barely open; in others, it will twist awkwardly. Seek the place where it stretches just right and looks balanced.*

- *Try combining the coil technique with others. For example, use it between a silhouette or tent pop-up and the backing sheet, or between a scenery flat and the backing sheet. The results can look spectacular and bizarre!*

Materials

*For **Coil Heart**, you will need*
- *Coil Heart paper elements*
- *Sturdy backing sheet (see page 16): 11" x 5" (28 cm x 13 cm)*
- *Covering layer: Medium weight yellow paper, 11" x 5" (28 cm x 13 cm)*

*For **Musical Score**, you will need*
- *Musical Score paper elements*
- *Sturdy backing sheet (see page 16): 11" x 6" (28 cm x 15 cm)*
- *Covering layer: copy paper, 11" x 6" (28 cm x 15 cm)*
- *Coil: Enough photocopies of lines of music to make 14 pieces, each 5" x 1 1/2" (13 cm x 4 cm)*

Equipment

Craft knife
Glue
Ruler
Photocopier

Coil Heart

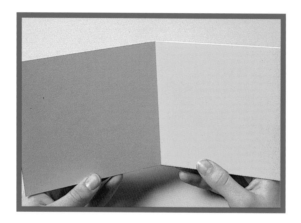

1 Make an 11" x 5" (28 cm x 13 cm) sturdy backing sheet.

2 Cut out the blue coil heart paper element, or create one using the templates and medium weight blue paper. Hold it so that the spiral coils counterclockwise from the edge to the center, then glue the end as shown.

3 Turn the coil over so that the glue is on the underside. Glue the coil into position on the backing sheet to the right of the gutter.

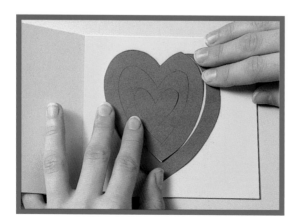

4 Glue the top surface at the center of the heart. Be careful not to let the glue spread beyond the center.

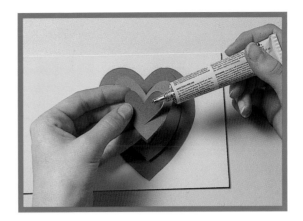

5 Fold the backing sheet in half, so that the center of the heart glues onto the left-hand half of the backing sheet.

6 Open the backing sheet to see the blue heart uncoiling across the gutter. Cut out the red heart paper element—or make one using the template and medium weight red paper—and glue it onto the coils, so that it is prominently displayed.

Musical Score

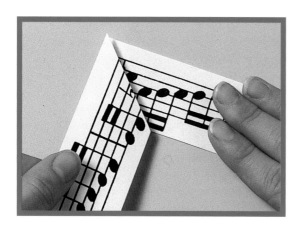

1 Cut out paper elements. Glue two pieces together as shown, ensuring that the angle between them is exactly 90 degrees. If you are using the paper templates to make this pop-up, make sure you you cut out twelve of the beveled shape and two of the rectangle shape.

2 Continue the pattern, gluing the third and fourth pieces into position. Once again, create exact 90-degree angles at the corners.

3 Glue together a total of seven pieces to form this square-section coil. The seventh piece is one of the two rectangular paper elements, used to create a flat end to the coil.

4 Turn the coil over. Glue the remaining seven units exactly onto the back of the first seven so that the musical score runs along both sides of the coil.

5 This is the completed coil. If the back-to-back gluing of the pieces looks a little ragged, trim the edges to neaten the effect.

6 Make a sturdy backing sheet. For the covering layer, two additional rectagular lines of music have been supplied. Place them an exact distance apart. That distance is the same as the distance between the lines of music along opposite edges of the square coil.

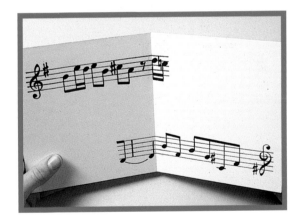

7 Glue one end of the coil to the backing sheet, so that the music flows uninterrupted across the join. Then glue the top surface of the other end of the coil and close the backing sheet over it, so that the glued end sticks to the backing sheet. If your measurements at step 6 were accurate, the music at this end of the coil will exactly join up with the music on the backing sheet.

Coil Pop-Up Gallery

Fireworks

The three firework rockets are glued to those parts of coils that stand vertically, so that the rockets themselves will also stand vertically, like the Coil Heart. The bright colors were achieved with oil pastel and glitter.

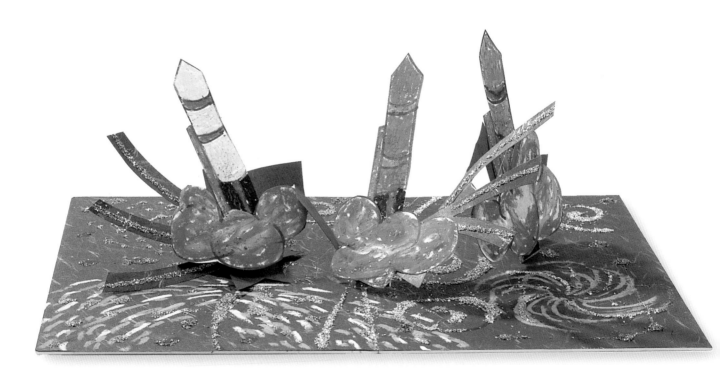

Soccer Kick

Again, this design is essentially the same as the Aerobatic Plane. If soccer isn't an appropriate sport to depict, adapt the image to one that is more relevant, such as football, baseball, golf, cricket, volleyball, and so on.

Rollercoaster

This is essentially the same as the Aerobatic Plane, but with fewer rotations of the coil. Try changing the shape of the coil to achieve a different corkscrew effect, perhaps to mimic a real ride in a real theme park.

Aerobatic Plane

A pop-up design need not always stand up on a horizontal surface such as a desk or shelf. When appropriate to the design, it could hang on a wall! The coil here is similar to the square-sectioned coil used to make the Musical Score, but it's circular and thus requires considerably fewer pieces to make.

Paper Frog

Frogs and toads figure in many traditional tales and legends all over the world. Their amusing, odd shapes make them charming and sometimes irresistible. Frogs have been fashioned from every kind of material: gold, silver, semiprecious stones, wood, porcelain, fabric, plastic, and of course, paper. Some people like to collect frogs, others may keep at least one for good luck.

The Japanese word for frog is *kaeru*, which sounds just like the Japanese word for "return home" and can be taken to mean: "Hopefully you will return." A gift of the likeness of a frog means the same thing: Give these paper frogs to friends as keepsakes that invite a return visit; or as mementos to wish travelers safe return home.

Materials

- *Frog paper elements*

- *Scissors and/or X-Acto Knife*

- *Paste or glue stick*

- *Brush for applying paste*

How to Build a Paper Frog

The frog is easy to make and fun to decorate. Real frogs come in every color of the rainbow, so anything goes for paper frogs. Bright or drab, speckled or striped, these frogs will liven up a table, bookcase, house plant, or windowsill.

Printed paper, to make both pond frogs and tree frogs, is provided in the back of the book. Try your hand at decorating paper frogs with appliqués and paint. Finished examples in the showcase chapter show variations you can make with this pattern; you may also want to consult illustrated field guides on the subject of amphibians. This project can be adapted to make paper toads, salamanders, and beetles.

Design Tips

- *Use sharp scissors or an X-Acto knife with a fresh blade to cut out the paper pattern. This will give you cleaner edges and a better-looking model.*
- *When removing paper pieces, cut from the back side of the paper provided. Cut just inside the outlines, and fold exactly on the indicated crease lines.*
- *Use very dark paper decorated with acrylic-based, iridescent paint to make frogs that look wet and slick.*
- *Create unusual jewelry by making frogs from foil or heavy aluminum embossing-sheets and then backing with a brooch pin.*

1 Score or valley-crease along the dashed lines on the underside of the frog pattern. This will give the frog's back a rounded shape. You can vary the degree of roundness by changing the angle of the folds.

2 Cut along the dotted lines to release the hind legs.

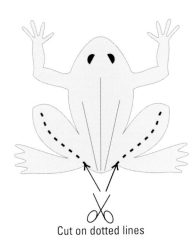

Cut on dotted lines

3 Valley-fold the front legs inward, horizontally across the underside of the pattern.

4 Valley-fold the front legs at a downward angle away from the shoulder area.

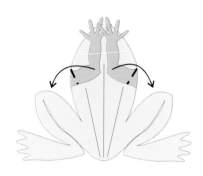

5 Form "elbows" in the front legs by mountain- and valley-folding a V-shaped set of pleats, as shown. The completed folds will allow you to position the frog's legs in a variety of ways for a natural pose.

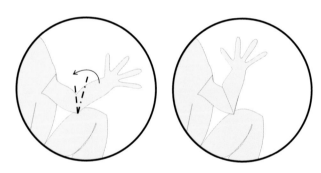

6 Using an X-Acto knife, cut a semi-circular line around the eyes of the frog. Turn the model over.

7 Fold the eyelids up, away from this side of the paper. You can shape the paper lids with a slight curve or roundness. Apply a small dot of glue to the heel of each of the frog's back feet.

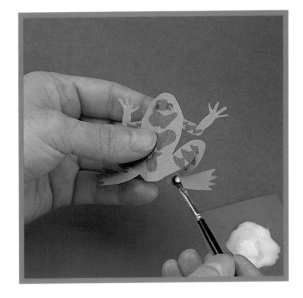

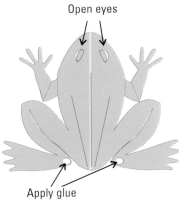

Open eyes

Apply glue

8 Glue the heels under the rump of the frog to make the hind legs rounded and three-dimensional. Valley-fold the hind legs at the waistline and adjust the all-over shape of the frog.

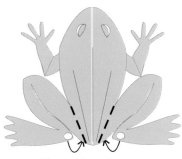

Glue heels under rump

9 The finished frog.

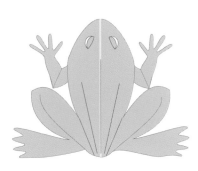

Paper Koi

In Japan, the carp symbolizes strength. Colorful kites resembling carp are hoisted each year in celebration of Boy's Day, a national Japanese holiday. The Japanese treasure the beauty of carp, and have traditionally bred many beautiful ornamental varieties, called koi. Today, people all over the world are discovering the beauty of koi—raising them in aquariums, garden pools, and simple backyard ponds. Any garden is greatly enhanced by a contemplative pool stocked with healthy koi. You can stock an indoor garden with these charming paper substitutes until the real ones arrive.

Materials

- *Koi paper elements*

- *Scissors and/or X-Acto Knife*

- *Paste or glue stick*

- *Brush for applying paste*

How to Build Paper Koi

Koi are considered very intelligent and friendly fish, and koi fanciers have bred some exceptionally beautiful varieties. Since they are popular features of many public gardens, it is likely you will be able to find some live koi for inspiration.

With a few sheets of paper and some paint you can create your own paper koi pond at home. Decorating paper koi with signature patterns of crimson, black, and gold is nearly as much fun as building them. You can paint the paper before you cut out the pattern, or you may prefer to compose the design on a finished, blank paper model. Either way you will want variety in the collection, so try both.

Design Tips

- *When pasting the rear ventral fins to each side of the keel in Step 4, keep the sides of the body, near the tail, rounded as you paste. The body will remain nicely rounded once secured in this way.*

- *When bending the head down in Step 6, remember to just hide the paper tabs with the gill covers—no further.*

- *When arranging groups of paper fish, curl the fins in a variety of ways, especially the tail fin.*

- *If you want to paint your koi, construct them from very white, slightly absorbent paper, such as watercolor paper. Apply paint with a light touch.*

1 Use an X-Acto knife to cut carefully on the dotted lines for the gills and center slot of the koi. DO NOT cut on the dashed lines.

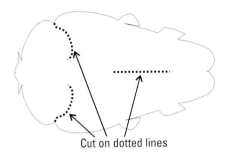

Cut on dotted lines

2 Mountain-fold the fins flanking the paper shape, as shown, and valley-fold the middle from the back end to the center slot.

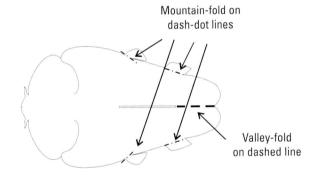

Mountain-fold on
dash-dot lines

Valley-fold
on dashed line

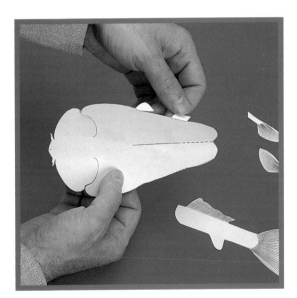

3 Apply paste to both sides of the indicated keel of the fin, as shown. Keeping the body paper flat, slip the top (dorsal) fin through the center slot that you cut in Step 1.

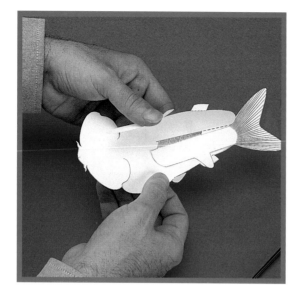

4 Fold the koi body paper in half and over the fin assembly. Keep the sides of the paper somewhat rounded as you attach the small, rectangular set of fins to the pasted keel. Carefully check the appearance of the koi at this point. The body should be conical and trim.

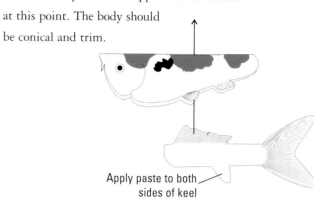

Apply paste to both sides of keel

5 Trim any excess keel paper protruding from the pasted fin area. Fold back the rounded tabs near the gill covers, as shown.

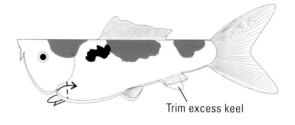

Trim excess keel

6 Apply paste to the outside of the folded tabs and bend the head just enough to attach the gill covers to the folded tabs.

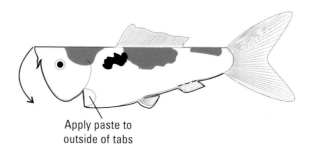

Apply paste to outside of tabs

7 The effect is a graceful, rounded fold for the slope of the koi's head. The gills should stand slightly open.

8 Apply paste to the tabs of the pectoral fins (they are labeled) and attach them to the inside walls of the open front, below and just behind the head. You can adjust these fins to any position that suits you.

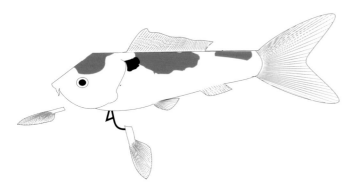

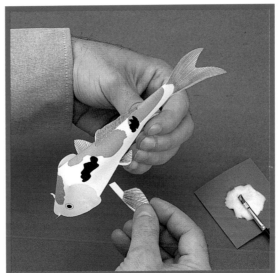

9 The finished koi.

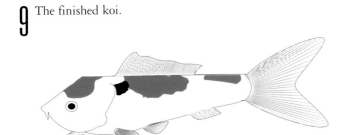

Paper Gliding Bird

P aper gliders become even more fun when you can take pride in the fact that you have built them yourself. Kites and toy gliders come in all shapes and colors, but none are more inspiring than those that resemble some wonderful bird, plying the winds and seeming to come to life in the breeze of a sunny day.

When building a new glider, always take care to fold very neatly. The number one axiom for best flight performance is balance! Once you understand the basics of good flight performance, you will want to make flocks of new flying creatures. Experience is the best teacher. Don't waste any more time—test your wings!

Materials

- *Gliding bird paper elements*

- *Scissors and/or X-Acto Knife*

- *Paste, glue stick or tape*

- *Brush for applying paste*

How to Build a Paper Gliding Bird

This graceful glider is a fun to make and even more fun to fly. Use the gliding bird as a party favor, or build a mobile and display a whole flock. Quick to make from any kind of paper, lightweight paper makes the best gliders.

Once you master the simple method of construction, you can adapt this pattern to make gliders of your own devising. The front edges of the wings are thick, folded layers of paper for stiffness. The body of the bird also has layered folds, to weight the front and to provide stable seating for the wings. Paste or glue is not needed for assembly, but we recommend it for permanence.

Design Tips

- *Be sure to cut neatly to preserve the symmetry of the wings. The wings control the bird's balance during flight.*
- *For faster flights, weight the front of the bird by adding a few pieces of tape.*
- *Before launching, check that the wings and tail are evenly set and without any twists or dents.*
- *Small birds, made out of reasonably stiff paper, fly the best. Experiment with different launching techniques. Basically, any way that you are able to get this bird into the air should produce a gliding flight.*

1 Begin by valley-folding the leading edges of the wing
paper to make them dense and rigid. You should fold the
narrow, flanking edges first, then the two large center areas.
The larger edges will overlap the smaller edges and hold
them in place. You can use glue or tape to keep the folded,
leading edges in place.

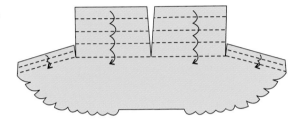

2 Valley-fold the outer wing areas, as shown. Mountain-
fold the center of the wing. The resulting M-shape of the
final wing will provide additional stability in flight.

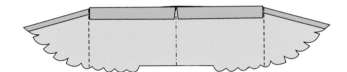

3 Begin to shape the body by mountain- and valley-
folding the part of the body strip closest to the tail.
Light-colored dashed lines are printed on the paper as a
guide. The result of the first two folds will look like the
figure in step 4.

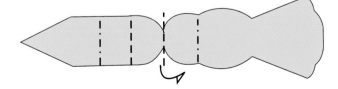

4 Valley and mountain-fold the remaining portion of the strip. The folds of paper at the front of the body provide the extra weight that will pull the model forward, through the air.

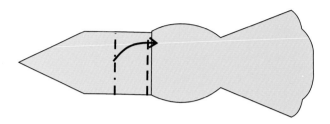

5 Mountain-fold the two indicated corners of the layered paper as shown, so that they disappear under the square edge. This helps to lock these layers in place. Mountain-fold the tail edges to form the tail stabilizers.

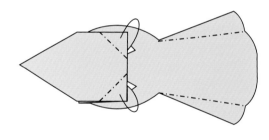

6 Form the bird's head and beak area by mountain- and valley-folding the pointed end of the body strip. There is no ideal placement for these particular folds, so just use your judgment. Mountain-fold the smaller side corners, as indicated, to make the shape trim.

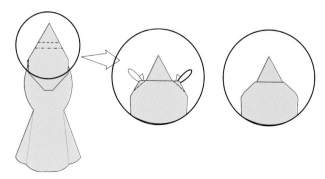

7 Valley-fold the body in half, lengthwise, to make a V-shape channel. This channel forms a stabilizing keel and a center valley to cradle the wings of the bird.

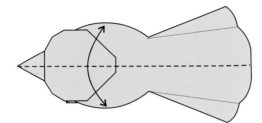

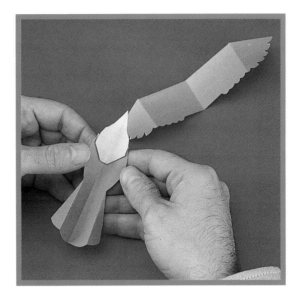

8 Insert the paper wings under the heavy folded paper edge of the head. You can use a bit of glue or tape to secure the assembly, but it is often not necessary if you have folded the paper crisply and neatly.

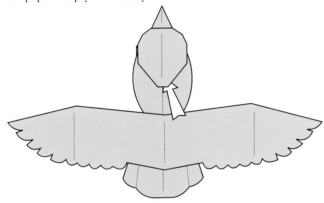

9 The finished gliding bird. To launch, hold on to the front center edge of the wing assembly and toss the gliding bird straight up, over your head in a backhand manner. The idea is to get the paper bird high in the air, where it will recover from a graceful loop and glide slowly to the ground.

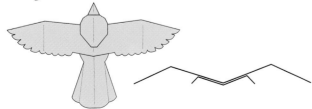

Paper Bat

Bats are certainly one of the most amazing and misunderstood of mammals. Perhaps it is their secretive, nocturnal habits that cause concern, or maybe it is their odd form. One need only take a closer look at these wonderful animals to begin to like them. Fortunately for bats and people alike, society is realizing the important role bats play in nature: Insect-eating bats help keep bug populations down; and pollen-eating and fruit-eating bats are vital to many plants. Many people have even built bat-houses to offer roosting sites for mosquito-eating bats. Paper bats are less intimidating than the real models, though not as effective against insects.

How to Build a Paper Bat

I n China, the bat has long been a symbol of good luck. The image of the bat is a popular motif in oriental pottery, fabric and building decoration. A dwelling with bats is considered fortunate.

The origami bat is the most challenging of the projects in this book, but it is worth the effort. This sought-after design is very popular: Even people who don't find the image of a bat endearing warm up to these charming fellows. It is also, of course, the perfect Halloween decoration or package ornament.

Materials

- *Bat paper elements*

- *Scissors and/or X-Acto Knife*

- *Paste or glue stick*

Design Tips

- *Always use paper that is the same color on both sides. If you have square origami paper that is colored on one side and white on the other, simply fold it in half, corner to corner, with the color on the outside; you will now have a triangle of the proper dimensions and colored on both sides.*

- *If you are using heavyweight paper, dampen it first with a sponge and then fold; when the paper dries, the folds will remain. Wet-folding is also a good way to add expressive touches to your work.*

- *Make a small hole in the center of the top of the head and add a loop of thread to make bat ornaments.*

- *Experiment by modifying the wings, ears, and faces of these bats, to make models that are large and scary, or small and delightful.*

1 Cut a square of paper diagonally in half, to make a
triangle of the proper proportions to begin this project.
This correct type of triangle has one square corner and two
45-degree angle corners. Any size will do.

      Valley-fold the triangle in half by bringing the two
45-degree angles together as shown. Unfold. This creates a
centerline. Valley-fold all three corners to meet at the end
of this center line where it touches the center of one of the
triangle's sides. Unfold. You will now have a set of valley-
creases, as pictured.

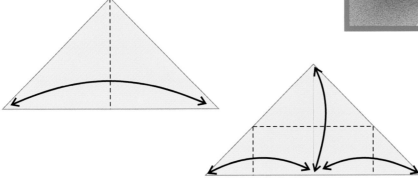

2 Valley-fold the two, 45-degree angle corners to the
square corner. Turn the paper over. Notice how this
square shape has two open edges and two folded edges.
Focus on the two folded edges of the square for the next
step: Fold each of these edges to the center line and allow
the triangular points from the underside to rotate around to
the front of the paper. The model should now resemble the
photo. Pay particular attention to the mountain-creases,
which bisect each of the triangular shapes in front.

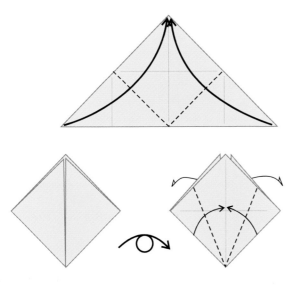

3 Grasp one of the mountain-creases, align it with the center of the model, and valley-fold the paper between the mountain-crease and the center line of the model. Do the same with the other mountain-crease. Mountain- and valley-fold the resulting paper triangles. Again, the model should resemble the photo. Turn the model over.

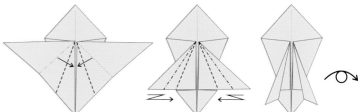

4 Check to be sure that you have the correct side of the paper by looking at the center line: it should be a valley-fold. Open up the model, then valley-fold the top corner to the center of the bottom edge of the model. Valley-fold this square corner piece way back, toward the top of the model. Notice the black dots at the end of the crease lines in the diagram. Align the end of each of the two crease lines with the folded edge of paper on their way up (dot-to-dot in the diagram). This will show you how far to fold the corner back up.

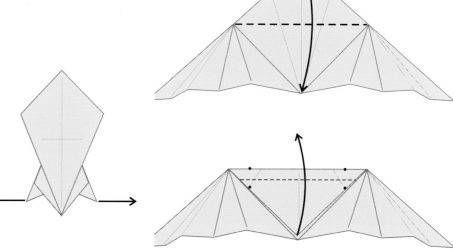

5 Create a scalloped edge along the bottom of the wings by setting in the indicated mountain- and valley-folds (optional). Mountain-fold the left and right arm-edges (see the circle diagram for detail) under and out of sight.

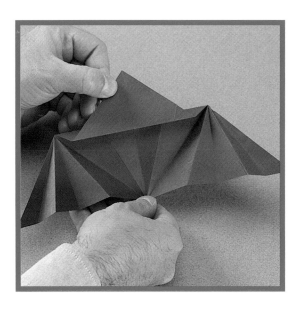

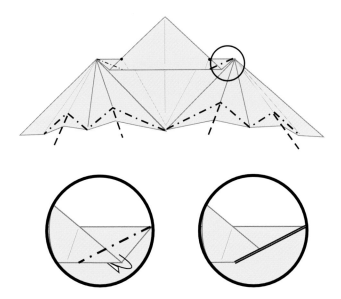

6 Mountain- and valley-fold the top corner to make the nose and head. Fold the nose first and then valley-fold the whole shape down. Fold the wings closed over the body. Use the diagram in Step 7 as a guide.

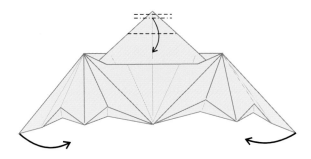

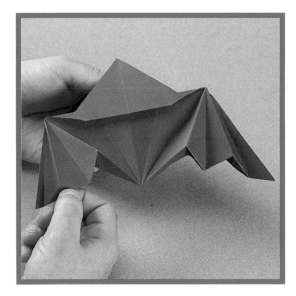

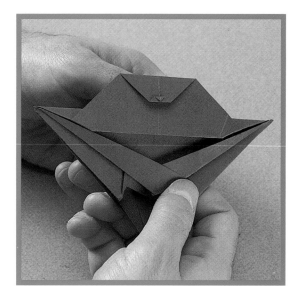

7 Mountain-fold the arms in half, lengthwise, beginning from the corner point and working inward until you hit a mountain-crease in the area of the body. Swing this mountain-crease up to touch the nearest ear corner and valley-fold the paper between them.

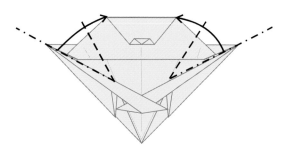

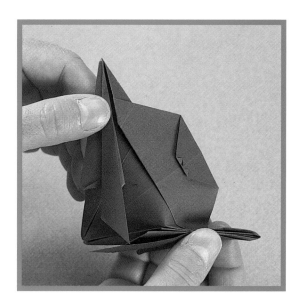

8 The folding of the previous step defines the head area and supplies material for shaping the features.

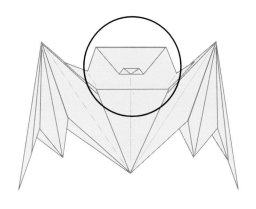

9 Mountain-fold along the paper edge that runs from ear point to ear point. Valley-fold the two ear points across the top of the head and make them stand straight up.

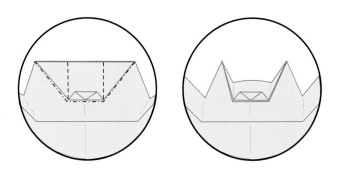

10 Twist the ear points so that the flat sides face forward (optional). Open the mouth using a toothpick or similar tool (also optional).

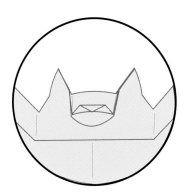

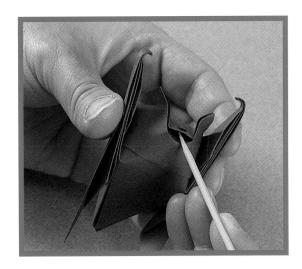

11 Open the wings out and tightly curl the end of each wing around a toothpick to shape. You may wish to make a few roosting bats by folding the wings closed.

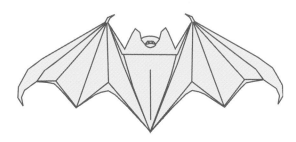

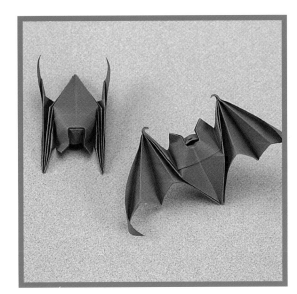

Paper Iris

Irises are related to lilies, and come in nearly as many shapes, sizes, and colors as do roses. Bearded iris, dwarf iris, Dutch, French, and Japanese irises, each has its own distinct appearance. To recreate irises in paper, use a paper with high rag content for bearded varieties, and a stiff, slightly shiny paper for making the crisp, dwarf varieties of iris. A quick glance at a garden catalog will supply enough color inspiration for a whole field of flowers: bright violet *Ruffled; Breathless,* with flamingo-pink blossoms; *China Maid,* petals in a blend of pink, buff, and lilac; *Crystal,* in bright, frosty blue; or *Frost and Flame,* pure white flowers with tangerine-colored beards.

Of the irises listed, dwarf irises are the easiest to mimic in paper, bearded irises are more difficult, and the Japanese variety is trickiest of all. Japanese irises are wide and flat, but soft in appearance. It takes careful planning to find (or adapt) paper that can be cut to so large a shape without excessive stiffness or without drooping under its own weight.

Materials

- *Iris paper elements*

- *Scissors or X-acto knife*

- *White glue*

- *Ruler or other straightedge*

- *Scoring tool*

How to Build an Iris

Named after Iris, the Greek goddess of the rainbow, this flower was the source of inspiration for the stylized fleur-de-lis design. Large and showy, the iris is an outstanding addition to any garden or flower arrangement, and a must on the list of paper flowers gathered for this collection.

The slim, graceful profile of the iris shows best when displayed as a single stem or in a small grouping of three. If you want to make a larger spray of flowers you will need extra leaves, or some more open paper flower-shapes, to fill out the bouquet.

The iris shown is a simplified rendition, requiring only a single piece of paper for the blossom. Although any color is suitable, remember that the iris is a spring and early summer plant. Paper in hues of pale pink and mauve, deep purple and lavender, or rich tints of yellow will offer the most natural-looking results. Once attached to its stem and leaf, the simple lines of this flower form become quite striking. Just a few of these blooms will add drama to any arrangement.

Iris Tips

- *For best effect, choose two-tone paper with a contrasting hues on either side. Use bright or dusty greens for the stems and leaves.*

- *A round pencil will curl flower petals better than a six-sided one; the facets leave unsightly horizontal rib marks.*

- *As noted before, the blossom is more durable if it is glued to the stem. Try to leave as little stem as possible showing inside the flower.*

- *When using the iris as the only flower in an arrangement, cut stems to varying lengths. Use iris leaves separately and insert into mixed arrangements of paper flowers.*

1 On the outside (light hue side) of the paper, mountain-
fold and unfold across gap notches between petals.
Repeat with the other two sets of opposing gap notches,
folding the shape in half three
times in this
manner.

2 Pierce the center to make a small hole for the stem.

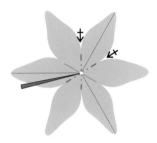

3 The blossom papers provided for this project have a line
dividing three of the petals in half. I will refer to this as
the centerline. Notice also that these three lines are arranged
in a symmetrical triangle. On either side of each centerline
is a mountain-crease. Fold each mountain-crease against and
aligned to its corresponding centerline. Repeat with the
other two sets of centerlines and mountain-folds. You will
end up with three petals on the outside and three petals on
the inside.

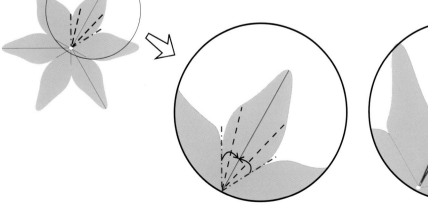

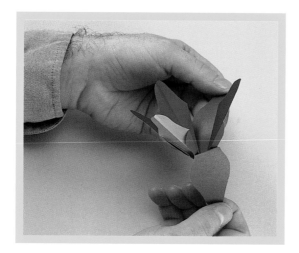

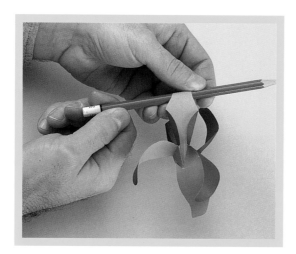

4 Fold down the three outside petals as far as they can go. Make a sharp, horizontal crease at the point where each petal attaches to the flower. Make sure all of the creases made thus far are very crisp.

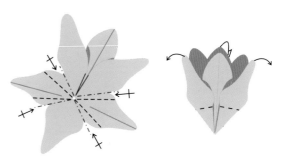

5 If your folding is neat and sharp, you will not need glue to keep the blossom in good form. Give the three outer petals a slight downward curl. Curl the three inner petals toward the center of the flower.

6 Make stems by folding the stem paper in half twice, lengthwise, to get a thin, four-layered paper spear. Two-thirds from the bottom of the leaf, fold the leaf in half lengthwise. You may then leave the leaf straight or gently curl it downward.

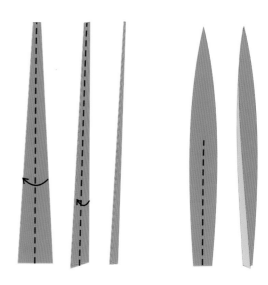

7 Insert the stem through the center hole from the bottom. Glue the leaf to the base of the stem. More than one leaf per stem and flower is a nice touch. You may also use iris leaves by themselves, to add green to other arrangements. Make extra leaves so that you can adjust the final composition of your flowers.

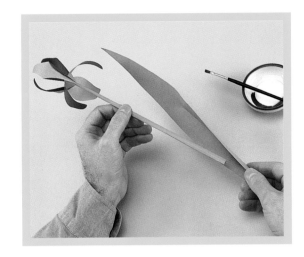

8 The finished iris—ready for display.

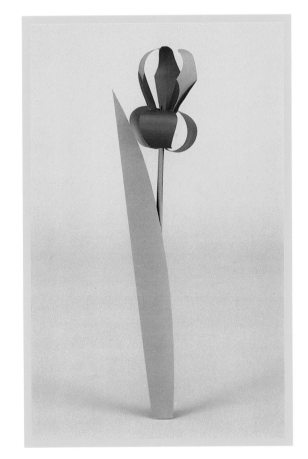

Iris Shortcuts

To cut folding time in half, fold two petal sets at once by stacking two cutouts together. Make sure all the petals are lined up and hold the layers firmly together as you cut. Make all the creases sharp and clean. Pull the two papers apart just before curling and shaping the petals.

Iris Gallery

Irises and leaves in a basket. The iris is a plant that carries itself well in a simple, uncluttered arrangement. A good balance of leaves supports the composition. If you stand the flowers up in aquarium gravel, the arrangement is easier to modify.

Long-stem vase arrangements can support more numerous blooms and a mix of colors. Long stems are best made from sturdier papers—or by folding more layers with lightweight papers.

Framed arrangements of irises and a paper butterfly make an elegant wall decoration. Choose a deep frame to emphasize the 3-D effect of the flowers.

Give gift packages oriental grace by wrapping them in handmade Japanese paper with iris ornaments.

To make your compositions dynamic, always use an odd number of blooms and keep them few in number.

Paper Posies

Posies are small wildflowers, such as buttercups, that bloom in the late spring and summer. Lady-smock and cuckoo-flower are traditional names for posies. Fields of posies growing wild are a sign of high summer in England. Common to grassy slopes, and growing in hues of silver-white, delicate pink, and rich yellow, posies—whether paper or perennial—look best arranged together in small vases, or in a small nosegay, tied-up with a ribbon. Without scent, but sweet in their appearance, posies suggest innocence and informality. Paper with a subtle sheen is best to reflect the silky, slightly waxy quality of posy flower petals.

How to Build a Posy

P osies can be a single, small, fragrant flower or a bunch of them. Posy is the informal name for wildflowers, gathered during a pleasant stroll and assembled into a spontaneous bouquet.

The posy selection here contains two types of small flowers: daisies and buttercups. Each is quick and easy to make—you can fill a May basket in no time. Do not hesitate to add these little paper flowers to any dried flower arrangement; they will fit in quite nicely.

Some paper butterflies are also included, to add to the effect of a bright, summer afternoon. You may wish to create your own butterflies by painting butterfly wing patterns on watercolor paper and using the cut-and-fold method as indicated on the pattern sheet.

Materials

- *Posy paper elements*

- *Scissors*

- *White glue*

- *Ruler or other straightedge*

- *Scoring tool*

- *Pencil (to open a hole in the base of the blossom)*

- *Toothpick*

Posy Tips

- *Choose colors typical of wildflowers, especially violet, yellow and white. Use drab or deep greens for the stems, to reflect that these are summer plants.*

- *The two-tone paper supplied for this project has a different color on each side. You can fold the project with either side outward.*

- *Add leaves from the other flower patterns in this book. Glue the leaves and blossoms in place for permanence.*

- *Tie together a bouquet of posies with ribbon and lace for a formal occasion or string them together to make garlands and leis.*

- *Cut butterfly shapes out of any brightly colored or patterned papers. Butterflies make great accents to any arrangement. Use them to decorate packages or as a brooch.*

To Make a Buttercup

1 Following the lines indicated, score one side of the paper buttercup pattern. This will be the "show side". You may lightly pencil these lines in first if you are not sure you are clear on their arrangement. Turn paper over.

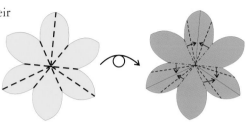

2 Fold the short creases (located between each petal) to touch and align with the long creases (running through the center of three of the petals). Notice that there are only three long creases and each long crease has a short crease on either side. If you fold correctly, the finished piece will look like an upside-down, conical paper cup. Turn the form over.

3 From this view you can see inside the buttercup—the three narrow petals will be very distinct. Using a pencil or toothpick, pierce a hole in the center. Do not make this hole too large—leave the paper snug enough for the stem to get a good hold.

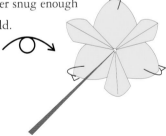

4 Make stems by folding stem paper in half lengthwise, twice, to get a thin, four-layered paper spear.

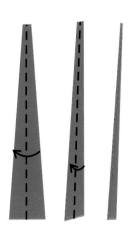

5 Insert the paper stem into the hole.

To Make a Daisy

6 Score or valley-fold creases up the center of each petal. Make sure that these folds are neat and crisp. Turn paper over. Score or valley-crease folds running straight between each petal. Again, be neat and crisp. Using a pencil or toothpick, pierce a hole in the center. Do not make this hole too large—leave the paper snug enough for the stem to get a good hold. Push stem paper through the center hole from the underside, working until the fit is very snug. Either side of the paper will work for the outside of the flower. You may also add the button center described in the Daisy project. Trim any excess stem paper from the flowerleaf center.

To Make a Butterfly

7 Mountain and valley-fold, as indicated in the diagrams, to bring the forewings to the hindwings (a). The forewings should overlap the hindwings slightly (as they do in real butterflies). Mountain-fold the center of the butterfly's body. Valley-fold along the body and wing attachment lines to bring the wings into a natural position (b).

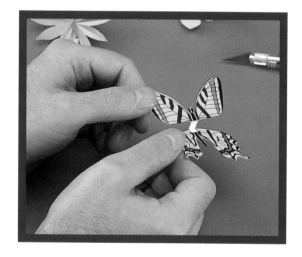

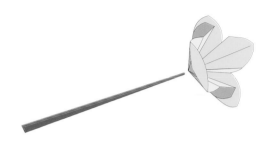

8 The finished butterfly. Add a butterfly or two to any summer bouquet of flowers.

9 Cut out the paper vase elements in the back pocket of this book and valley-fold on the dashed lines. Paste tab (a) to inner edge (b) and tab (c) to inner edge (d). Place the completed vase over a small can or plastic drinking cup and fill with paper flowers.

10 The completed project: paper vase, posies, and butterfly.

Posy Shortcuts

Save time cutting out flowerleaf elements by stacking up four sheets of colored paper and cutting them all at once. Trace the outline of the template onto the top layer of the paper stack, then cut. Be sure to keep all of the paper layers tightly together as you cut.

Posy Gallery

Coffee cake garnished with daisy and buttercup blossoms. Use paper posies to garnish all types of salads and desserts.

A May basket filled with posies is a delightful project for young and old. The basket is a simple, construction paper cylinder wrapped around a paper cup. The edges of the basket were made fancy with scissor-cut fringe. A long strip of construction paper makes a good handle.

Posies arranged in a simple pitcher. A cheerful accent piece or gift. Make longer stems and create colorful arrangements in any container.

String together buttercup blossoms to make a lei or garland to grace an item or a setting. A needle and thread make quick work of this lovely floral accent piece.

A gathering of paper posies makes a fine nosegay. A ten-inch piece of green paper cut and folded in a buttercup pattern serves as collar and background to this hand-held arrangement.

Paper Lotus

How to Build a Lotus

Exotic and mysterious are the words traditionally used to describe the lotus or water lily. Lotus blossoms set against the dark and quiet water of a secluded pond are one of nature's most evocative and enchanting displays.

Although it appears complex, the lotus that follows is one of the easiest constructions in the book. It is also the most beautiful. You will be surprised at how effectively a single lotus blossom and lily pad can cast splendid spell. Arrangements of water lilies are perfect for dinner table centerpieces, the coffee table, or a display shelf in the book case. You can use your most elegant papers on this model. However, even plain white shelf paper will be transformed when you fold it into a lotus. Scale the pattern as large or as small as needed for your arrangement—or make the flowers more lush by adding extra layers of paper.

Materials

- *Lotus paper elements*

- *Scissors*

- *White glue*

- *Ruler or other straightedge*

- *Scoring tool*

- *Pencil*

Lotus Tips

- *Any color is suitable for the blossom, in nature lotus colors range from deep crimson to stark white.*

- *To float paper lotus blossoms, make thin wax floats by dripping melted wax onto a cold water surface. Place the floats on the surface of a punch bowl or beverage and rest the lotus blossoms on top.*

- *Use only food-grade waxed papers for lotuses to garnish food. Glue the flower elements together with drops of melted candle wax instead of paste or glue.*

- *Always use caution when working with melted wax and flame. Keep any candle flame away from paper ornaments.*

1 Score or valley-fold the center of each petal. Do this to all three pink sets of petals and both yellow sets. It does not matter which side of the paper you choose, so long as all the creases are valley-folds. The valley-fold side will be the inner side of the finished flower.

2 Valley-fold along the base of each petal. Do this to all three pink sets of petals and both yellow sets.

3 Apply a little glue or paste to the center of the underside (mountain-fold side) of each element and stack them one on top of the other as shown in the diagram. Be sure to rotate each petal set so that the petals from one layer show between the petals above it. Press together firmly and let dry. The petals in the center should be more tightly closed than outer petals.

4 Put a valley-crease through the middle of the lily pad. This will be the outer side of the leaf.

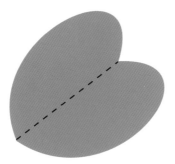

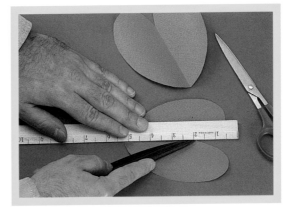

5 You may curl the outer edges of the leaves up or down for a more natural effect.

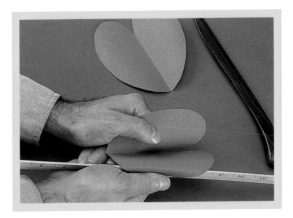

6 The completed lotus—ready for display.

Lotus Shortcuts

When making lotus from tissue paper or baking parchment, stack up to six layers of paper for each shape cutout. Trace the template on the top layer of the stack and cut all six layers at once. You can also fold up to three layers at a time.

Lotus Gallery

A lotus and paper frog in a display setting. (The frog project is featured in *Paper Animals*, book three in this series.)

Make a decorative indoor wreath of lotus and rose elements. Alternate color layers of lotus elements to support and frame each rose blossom. Secure each piece to a cardboard ring and a loop of cord attached to the back for hanging. A hot-melt glue gun makes quick work of the final assembly.

To beautify a formal dinner setting, use a paper lotus to fill each guest's empty plate. Each guest can then keep their lotus as a memento.

Float a lotus bloom in a punch bowl for an exotic touch. Make the blossom out of waxed paper or foil and set it on top of a wax float that is at least the diameter of the base of the bloom. Remove from bowl at serving time.

The lotus makes a wonderful table centerpiece because of its elegance and low height. You can also make blossoms to match your dinner napkins. Back fabric pieces with paper to make them suitably foldable. Practice on scrap material first.

Paper Rose

Although they are not as fragrant, paper roses last much longer than the real ones do. Since real roses come in all shapes and sizes, there is a lot of room for creative license when making a paper rose. Shades of red and pink are classic rose colors, but yellow, white, peach, and even near-black garnet, are all shades that can be found in real roses and that can be adopted for a bouquet of the paper variety.

If you like long-stemmed roses, such as tea roses, remember that they can look spindly on their own. Fill in your arrangement with shorter-stemmed primroses, or luxuriously petaled cabbage roses. Since roses have layers of beautifully unfurling petals, you will get the best results if you study a few real roses before attempting this project.

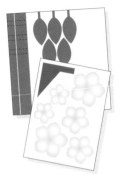

Materials

- *Rose template*

- *Scissors*

- *White glue*

- *Ruler or other straightedge*

- *Scoring tool (such as a letter opener)*

- *Pencil or toothpick (to open a hole in base of blossom)*

How to Build a Rose

The blossom shown here requires only four pieces to complete. You may scale the pattern down to create charming miniature roses, or make the scale larger for a more dramatic display. Adding paper stems and leaves (demonstrated on page 14) will make your flowers even more beautiful and lifelike. The rose pattern can be used as it appears, or adapted to create carnations by using pinking shears to cut the pattern from tissue paper. Double or triple the tissue for each layer of the blossom pattern, to provide extra petals and more support for the flower, then fluff open the layers after assembly.

Colorful fabrics make wonderful roses, too: if you lightly coat the back of the selected fabric with spray adhesive and apply a thin paper backing, the rose pattern will look like fabric and fold like paper. Use these fabric roses as coordinated interior accents.

Once you have mastered the folded rose by using the special pattern at the end of the book, try experimenting with other paper textures, colors, and patterns. This simple method produces stunning results from even the most ordinary paper. Try newspapers, magazine pages, or book covers; or use coupons, concert tickets, or seed packets—the list is endless. After a time, you may find yourself going beyond the scope of this book and applying the rose technique to create dozens of other plant and butterfly designs.

Rose Tips

- *Once all of the elements are cut out, clean the work area of any scraps of paper or debris that could later be confused with the actual flower cutouts.*
- *For maximum "grab", make only a small hole in the bottom of each part of the blossom, then let the paper stem enlarge the hole by itself.*
- *The leaves may be arranged any way that you feel looks best. Try making additional pockets and leaves, or skip the pockets altogether and glue the leaves to the outside of the stem.*
- *You may choose to glue the stem closed once the blossom is inserted. Blossoms and leaves can also be used alone, without a stem.*

1 Following the fold-lines, score the backs of petals using a letter opener and straightedge. Turn the paper over.

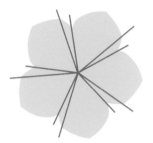

2 Make pleats, starting on the left side of the petal and working left to right. The score lines will guide you. Fold loosely at first, then tighten the entire piece to finish.

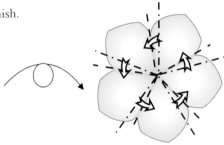

3 Fold each petal down, to make the shape pictured here. This fold extends only halfway across each petal. You may also curl the petals, for a softer effect.

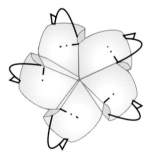

4 Pierce a small hole in the center of each unit (a sharp pencil works well for this); keep the hole as small as possible.

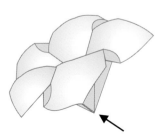

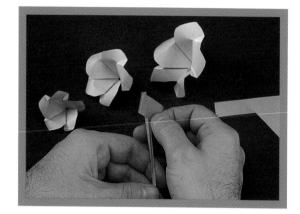

5 Make the center spike by repeatedly folding triangle in half (a-c). Be sure that your folds are tight and sharp. Curl the flag tightly around top of spike and make a cone shape (d & e). You may loosen this curled paper after the blossom has been assembled.

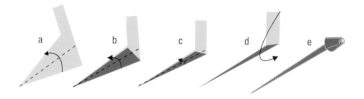

6 Assemble blossom. You may apply a small amount of glue where the petals meet the spike (optional, but recommended for permanent displays.) White glue works best.

optional glue points

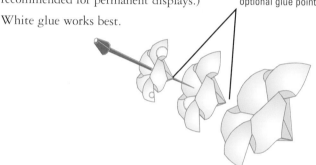

7 Fold each leaf in half, lengthwise. Make an angled crease as a guide. The angled crease sets the direction and spread for veins in the leaves. Make all creases sharp.

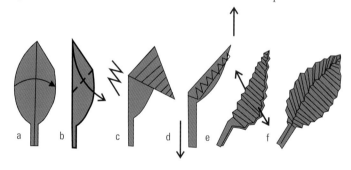

8 Next, tightly fan-fold the leaves. You may vary the width of each pleat, narrower toward the tip and wider at the center. Open out each leaf completely and shape it with your fingers. If you want to add a stem, follow the folding method shown in the line drawings below.

Fan fold

Fold and unfold   Fold edges to center

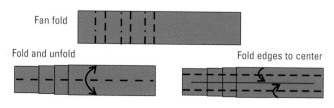

9 Insert leaves into stem. Be sure that you insert the leaves on the smooth, outside of the stem (side with no raw edges showing). Pay close attention to which side of each leaf is uppermost. Glue is not necessary here.

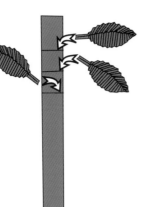

10 Fold the stem in half (lengthwise) once again, on the existing center-fold line. Hide the raw edges inside and narrow the stem.

11 Finally, insert the blossom into the top end of the finished stem. Choose a secure group of layers to do this. You may apply a small amount of white glue for permanence.

12 Perfect roses—ready for display.

Rose Shortcuts

You can skip the pocket folds when making the stems. Glue the leaves directly to the outside surface of the finished stem. Use only two petal segments for each flower; the top two together will make a small blossom, the bottom two—a larger blossom. Single petal segments (alone) make pretty apple or cherry blossoms.

About the Authors

Michael G. LaFosse has been designing, creating, and teaching origami for more than twenty years. Inspired when he was just twelve by the work of origami master Akira Yoshizawa, LaFosse began making and folding paper to create his own origami designs. Often sculptural, his work is not always immediately recognizable as origami. However, most pieces originate from a single square of uncut paper. Favorite subjects for LaFosse's origami are taken from nature: flowers and animals that he studies in their natural habitats. He often makes his own paper for these designs, imagining the paper as the "flesh" and the folds as the "bones", striving to create lifelike origami with all the character and attitude of the original subject.

How is it possible to convey nature's poetry and spirit within the folds of a single piece of paper? LaFosse's exquisite work shows that paper folding is a three-dimensional drawing process, and an art in and of itself.

Paul Jackson is a professional paper artist and paper engineer who has an M.A. in Fine Art from the University of London. He has written many books on pop-ups, origami, and paper sculpture, and lectures at art and design schools in the United Kingdom, Europe, and the United States. Jackson makes models commissioned by advertising agencies and design companies, and he exhibits widely.

Paper Elements and Templates

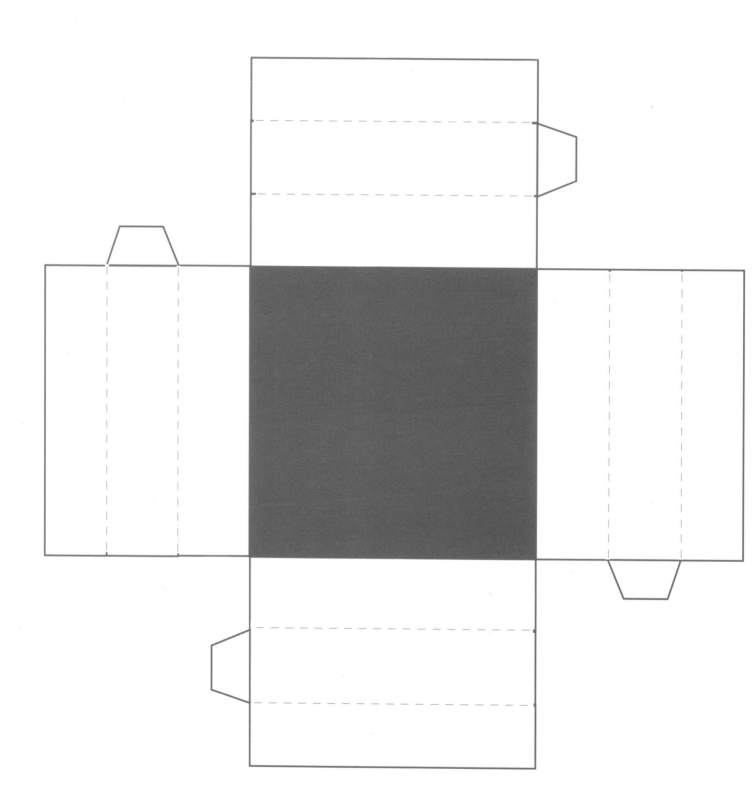

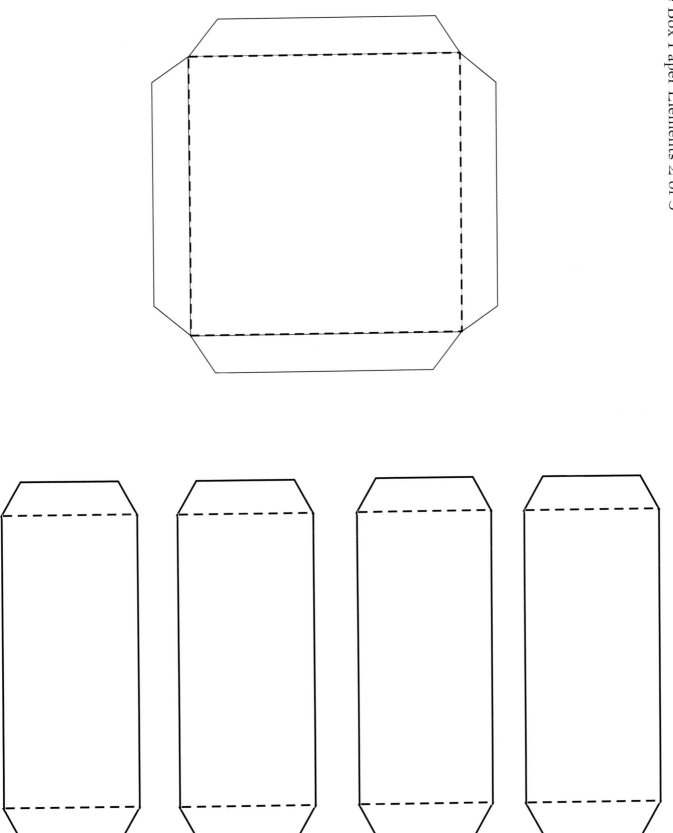

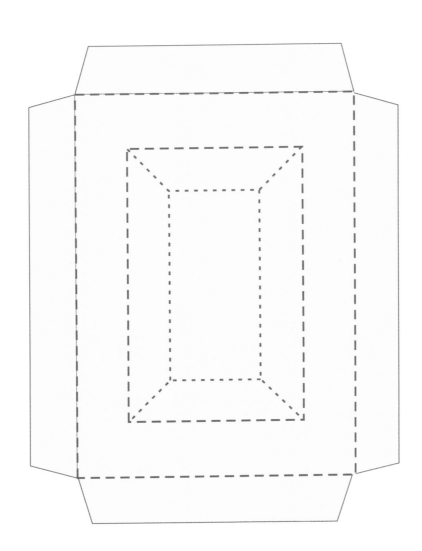

Puzzle Box Paper Elements 1 of 2

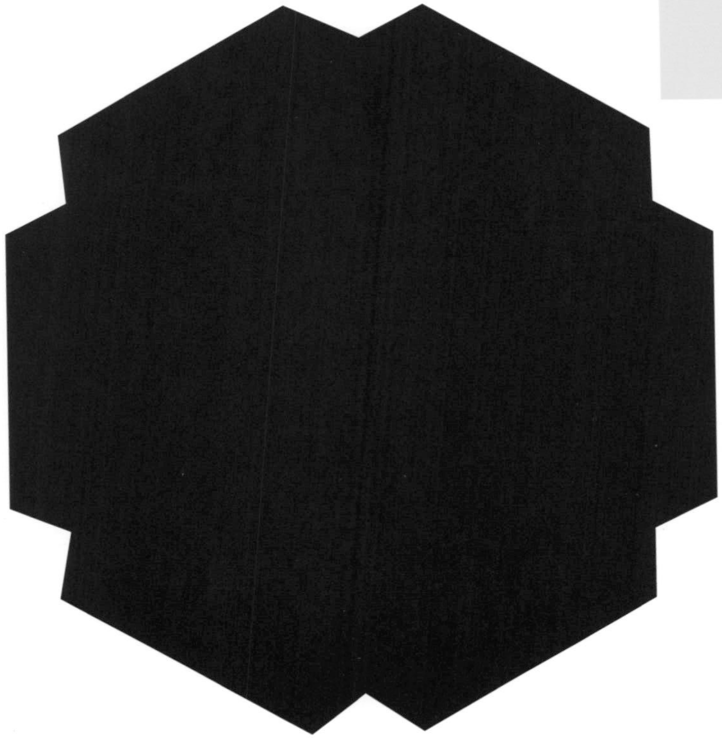

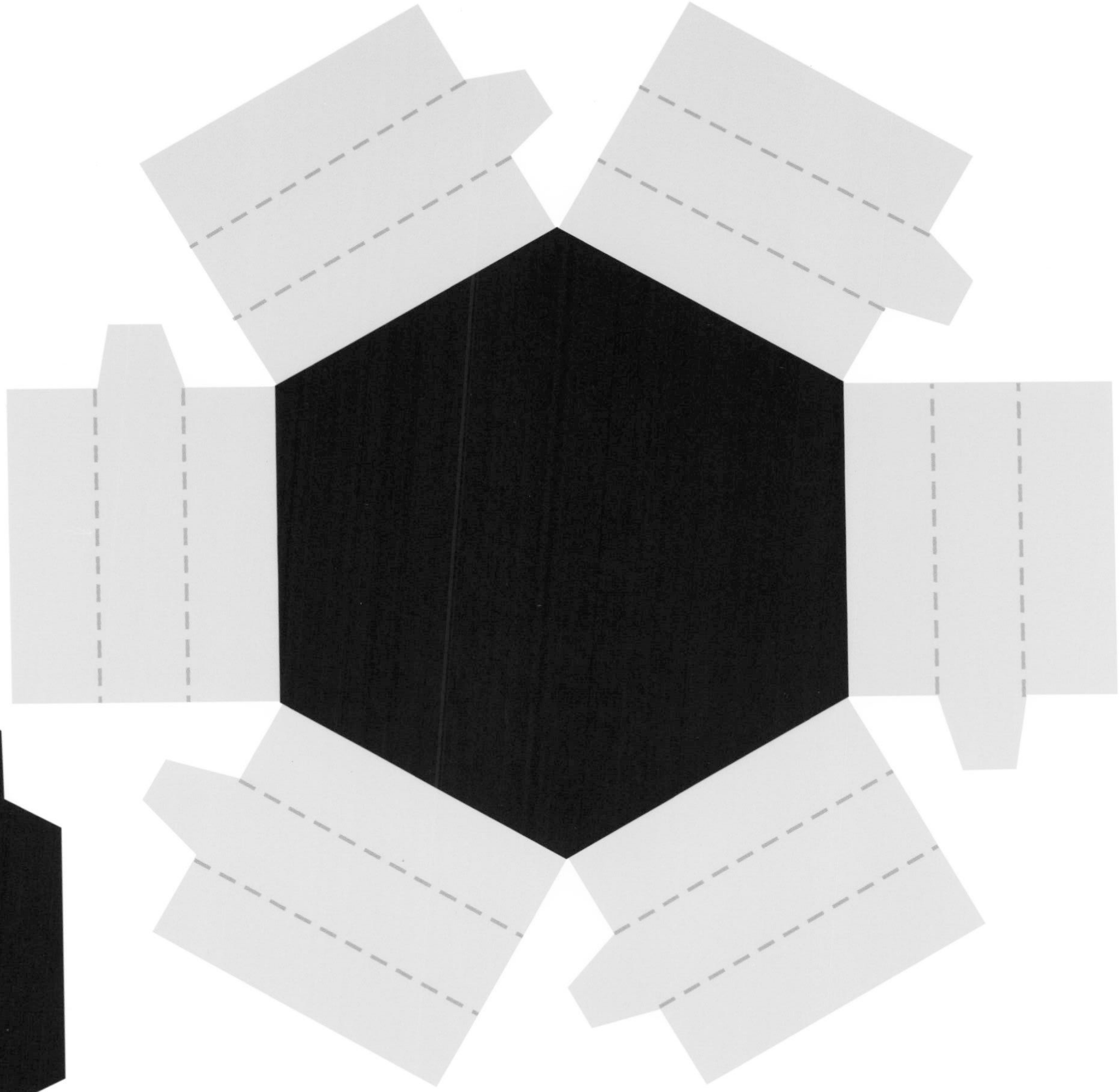

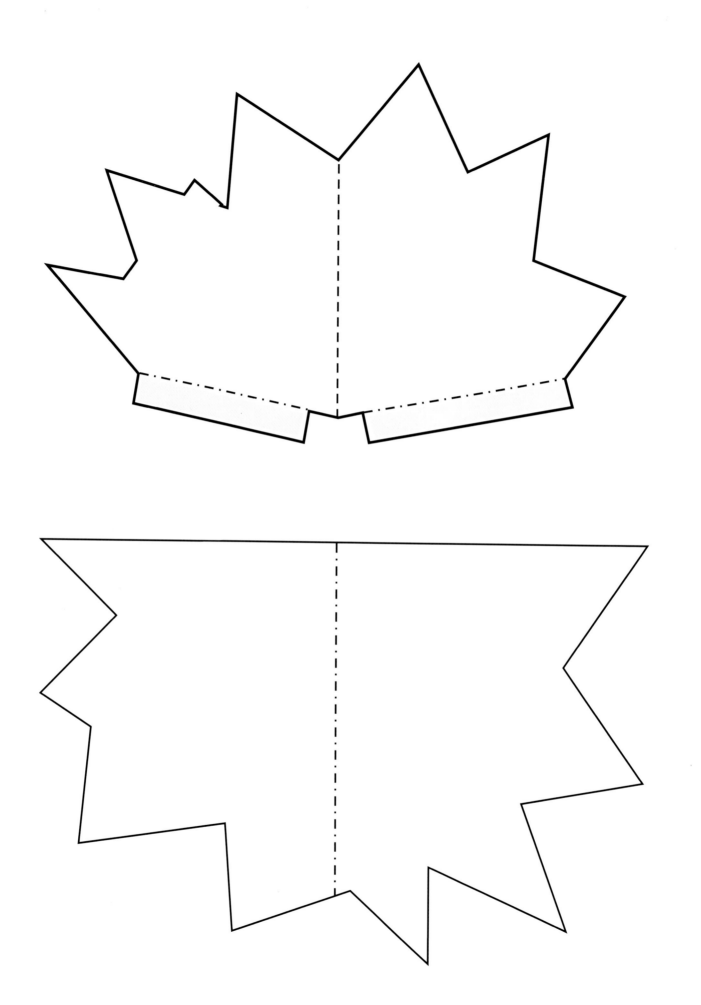

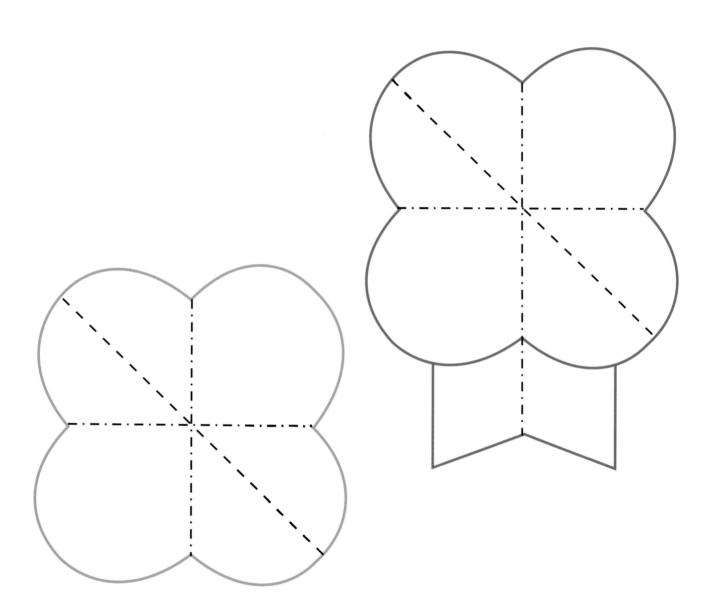

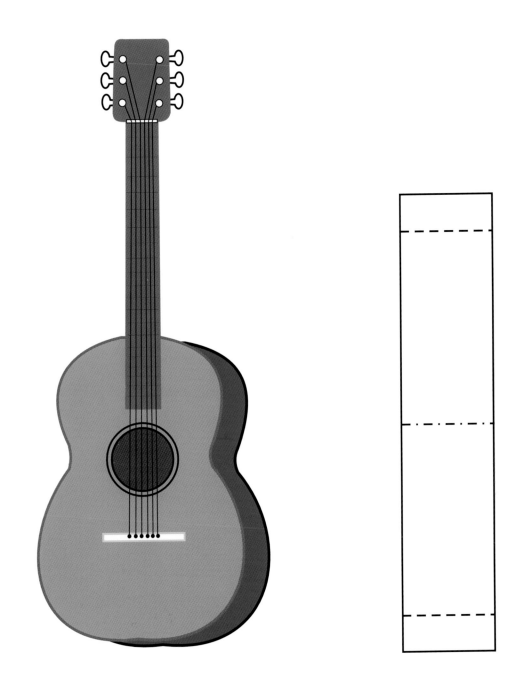

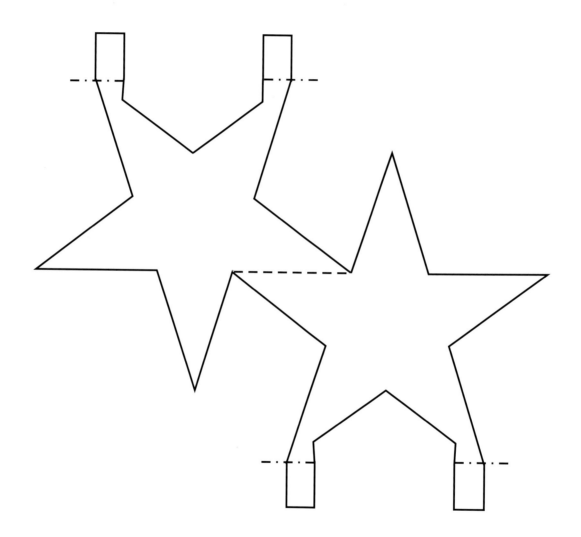

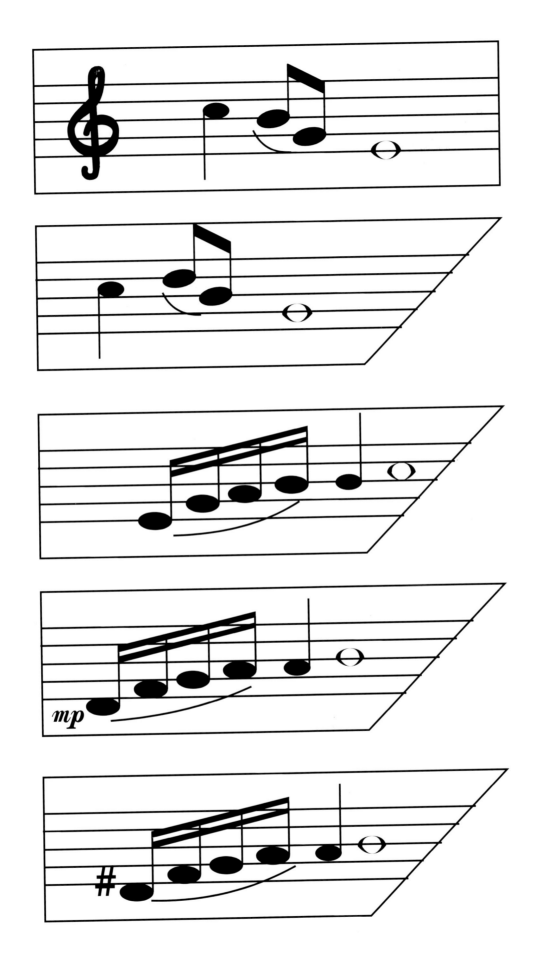

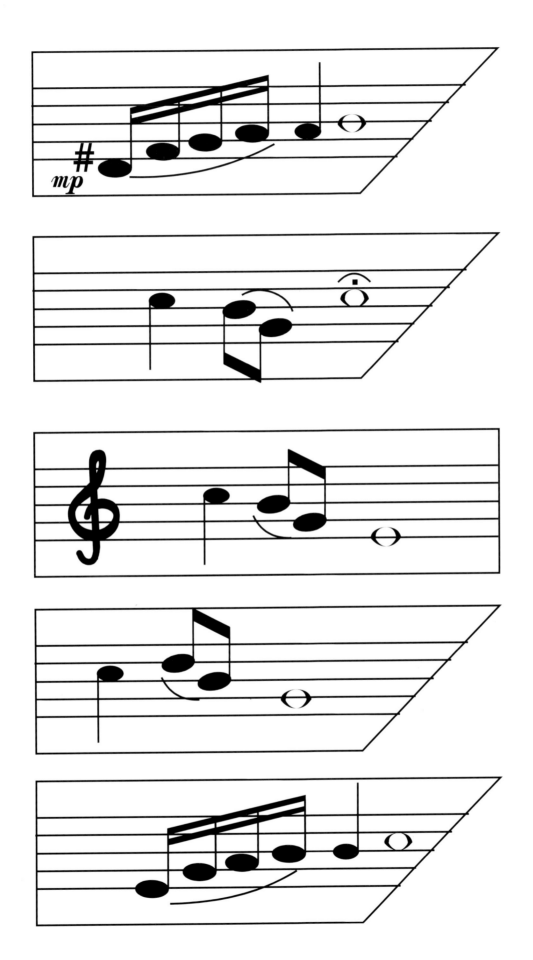

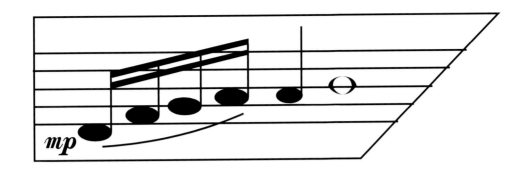

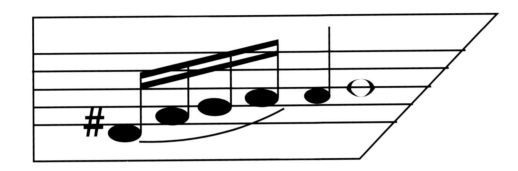

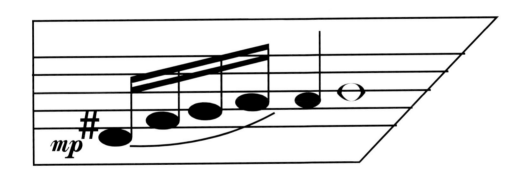

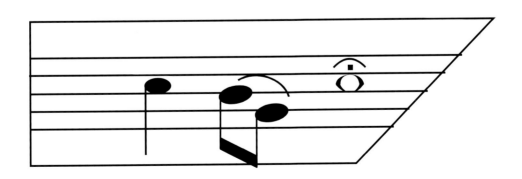

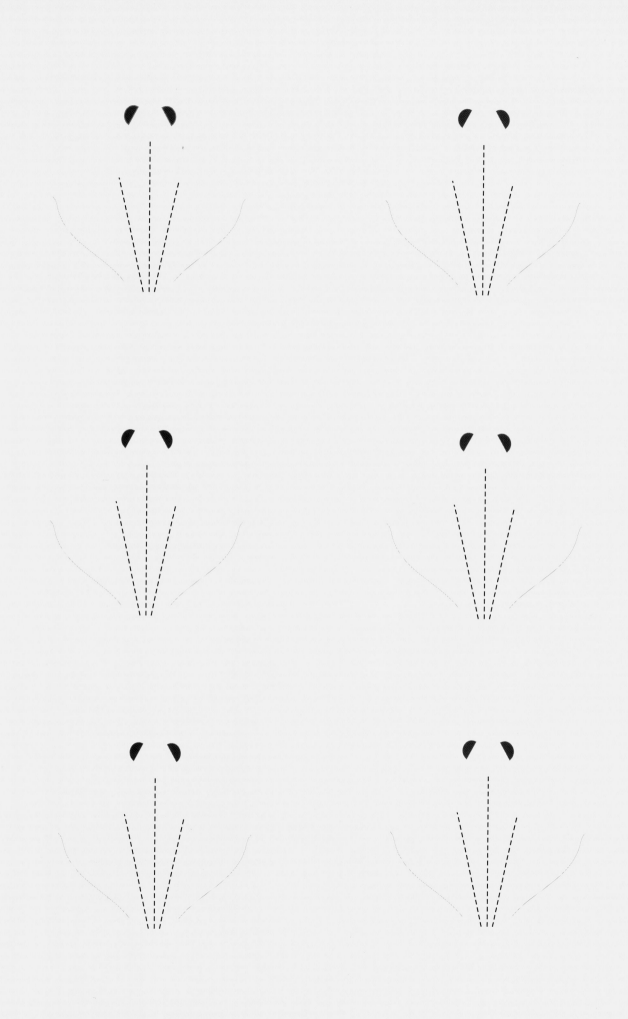

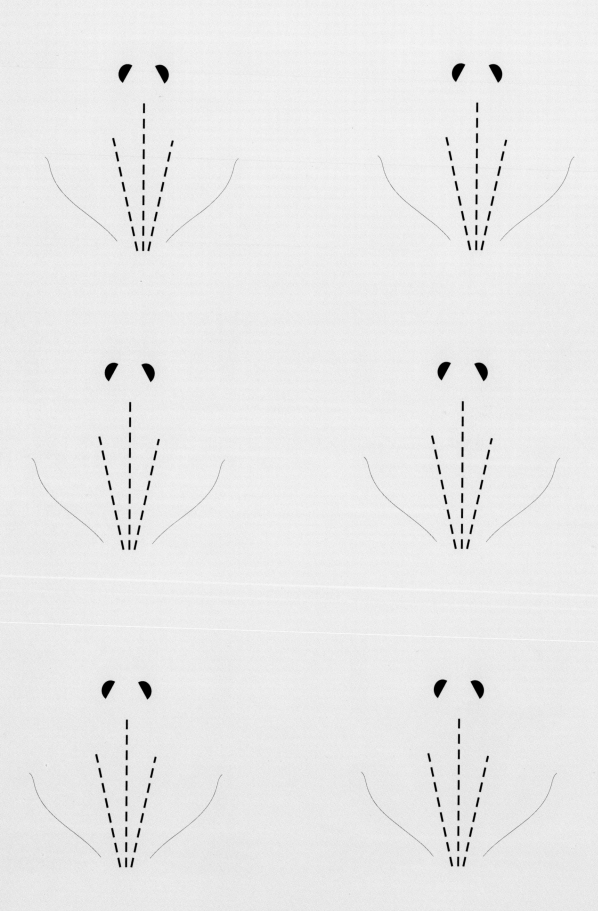

Iris Paper Elements – 1 of 2
To make two irises

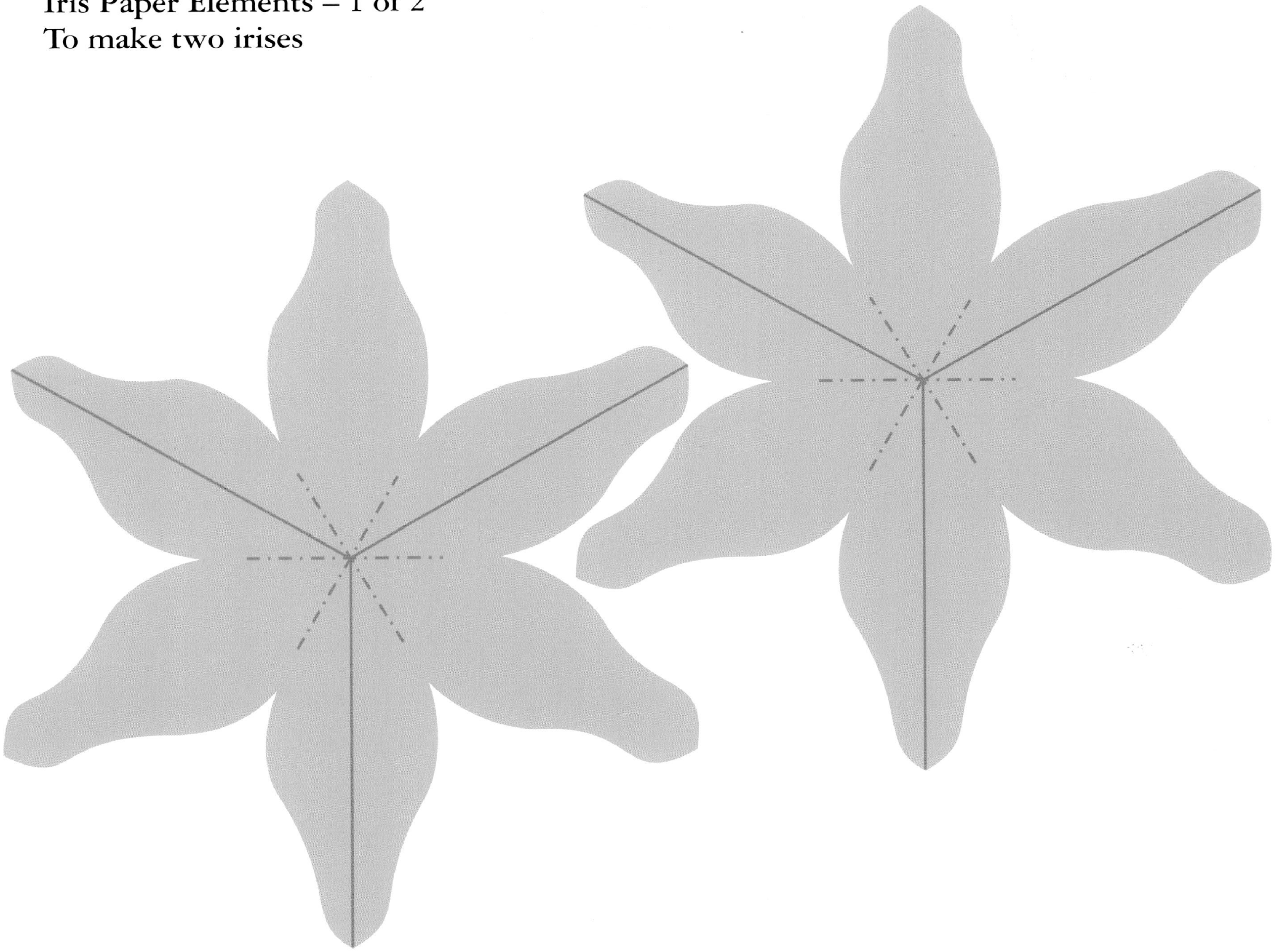

Lotus Paper Elements – 1 of 2

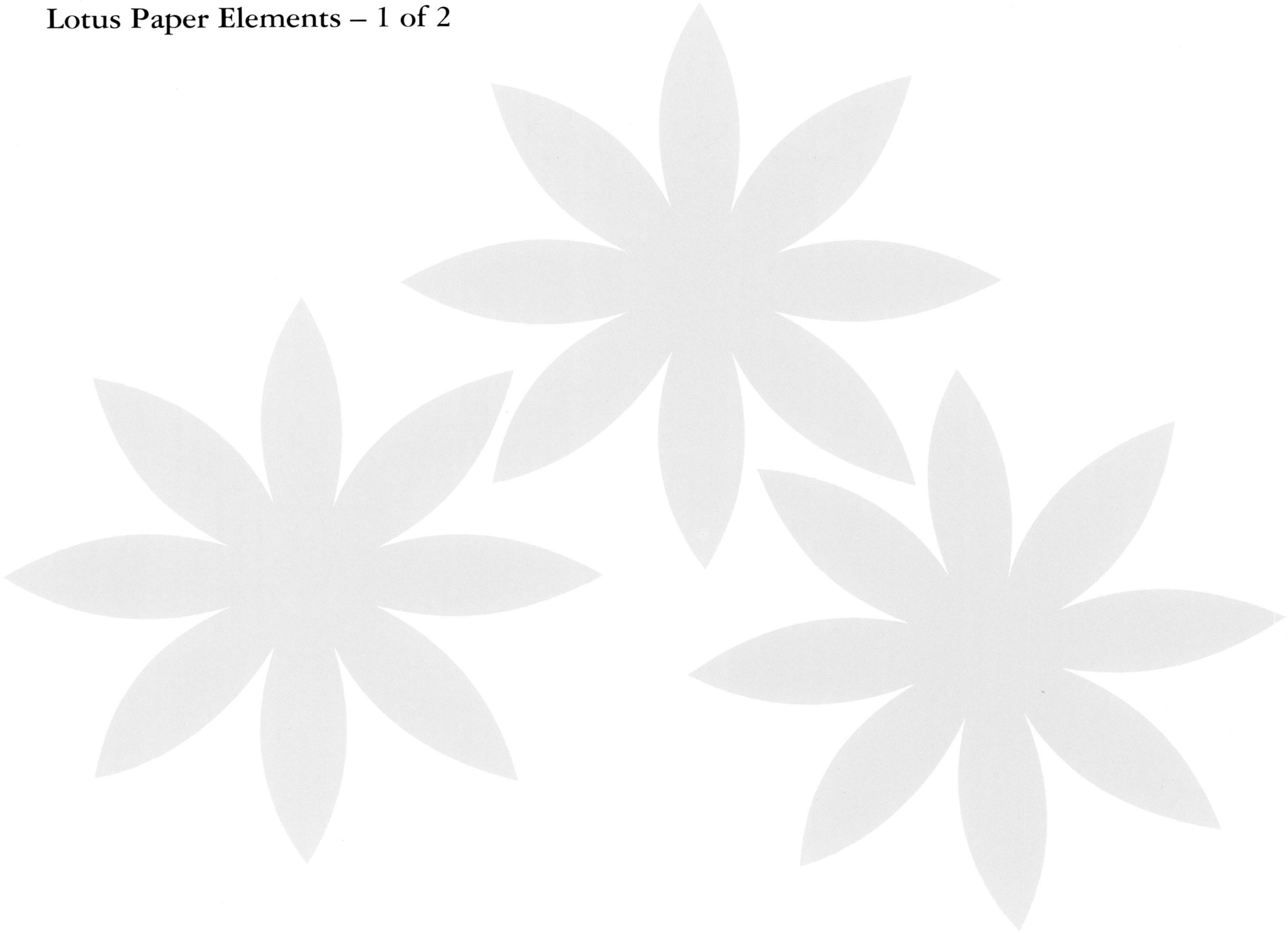

Lotus Paper Elements – 2 of 2

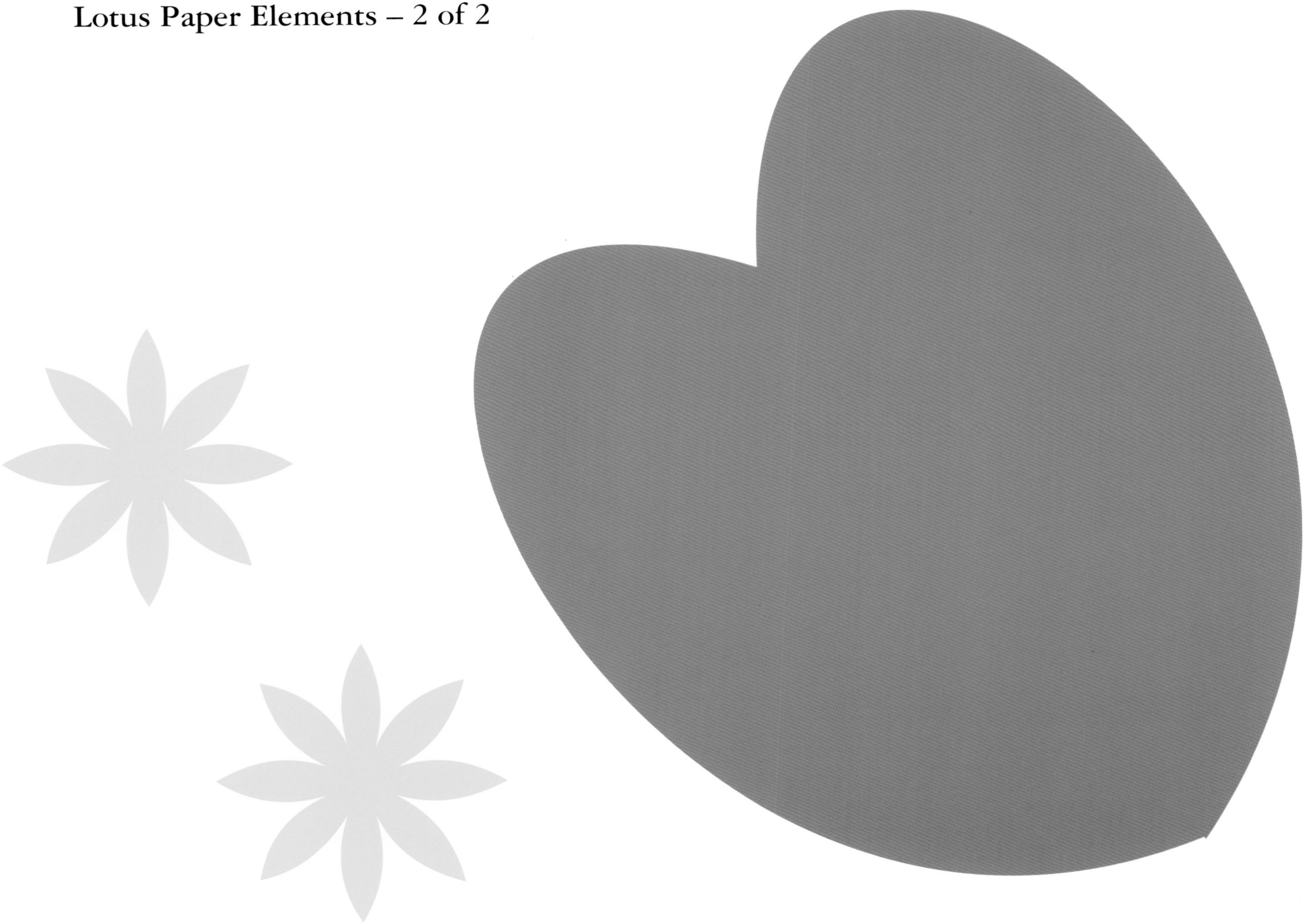

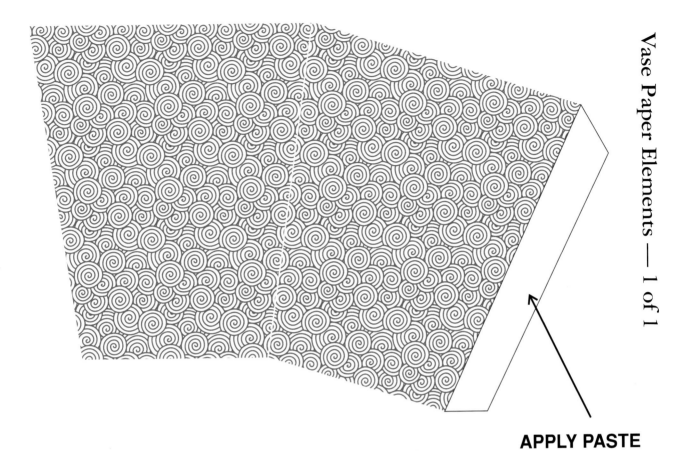

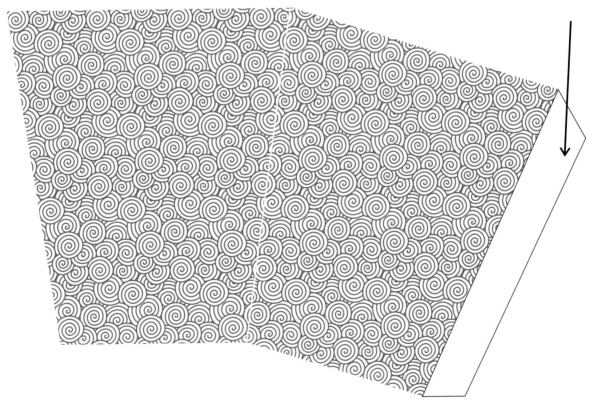

APPLY PASTE

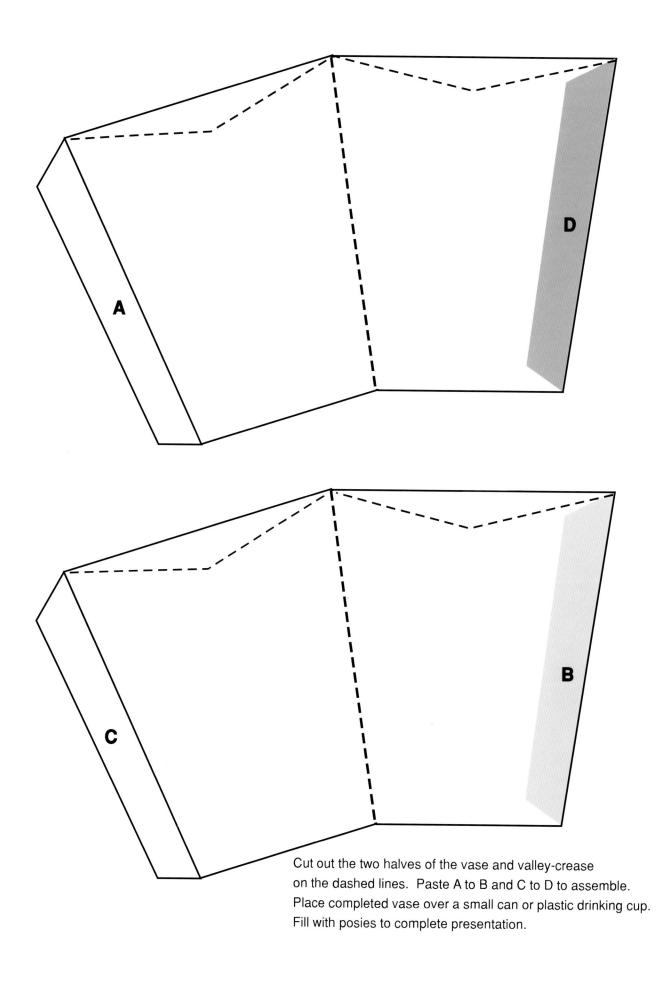

Cut out the two halves of the vase and valley-crease
on the dashed lines. Paste A to B and C to D to assemble.
Place completed vase over a small can or plastic drinking cup.
Fill with posies to complete presentation.

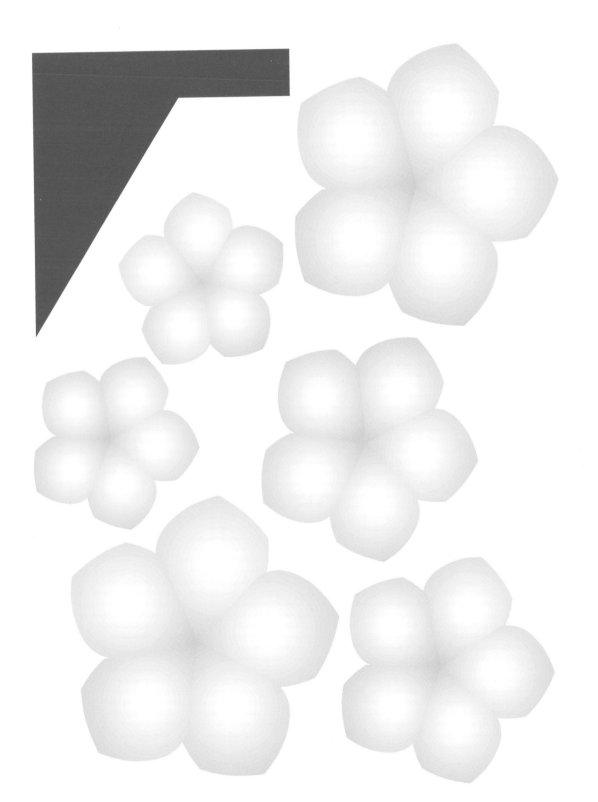

Rose Paper Elements – 2 of 2

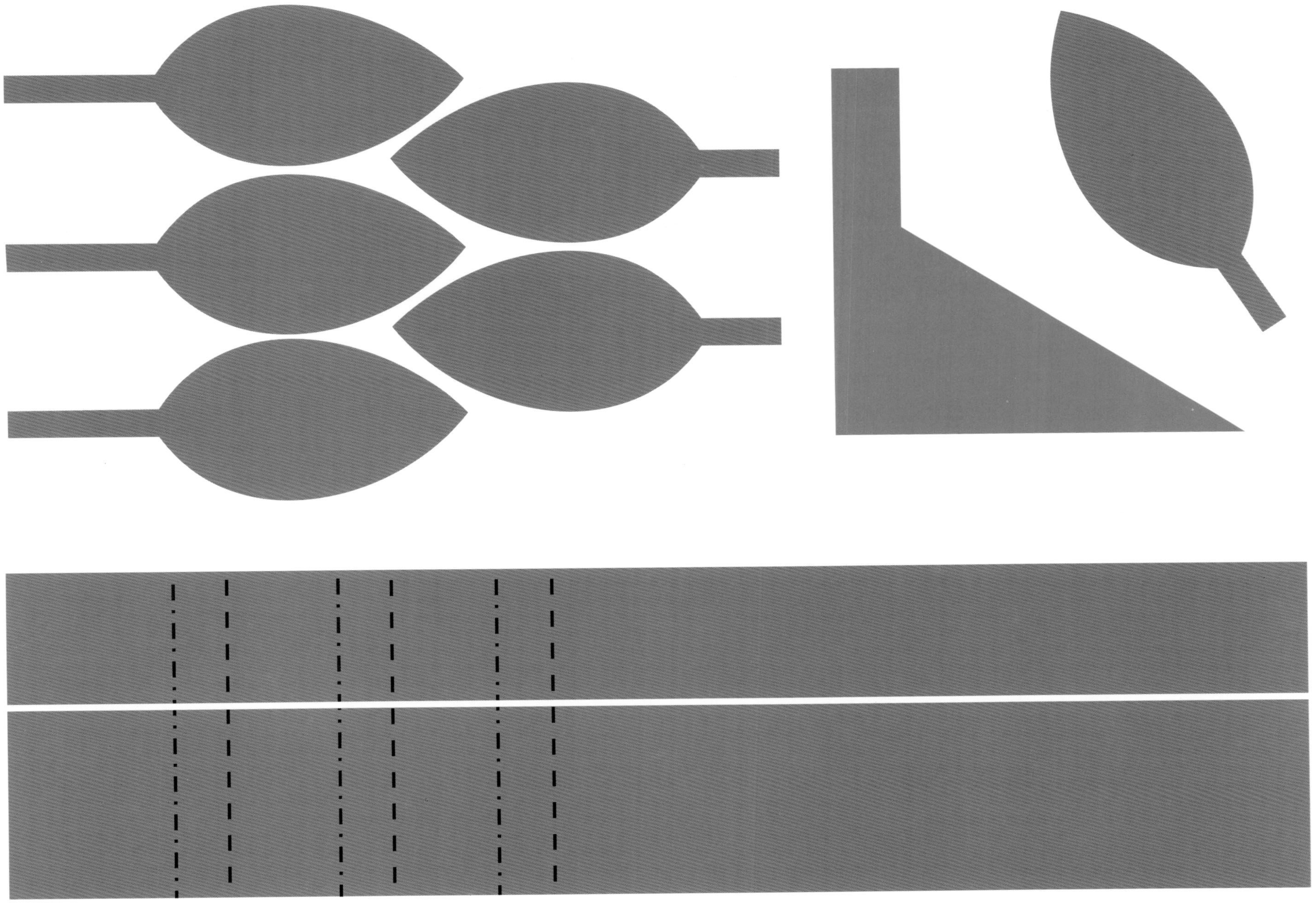

Cube Box
Lid

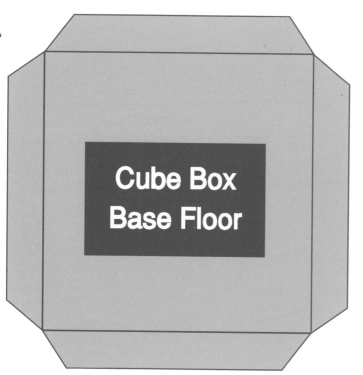

**Cube Box
Base Floor**

Cube Box
Lid
Strips
(Make 4
of 2
colors.)

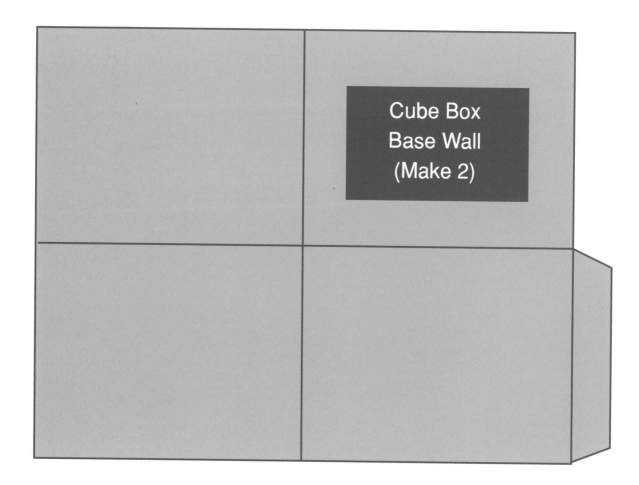

Cube Box
Base Wall
(Make 2)

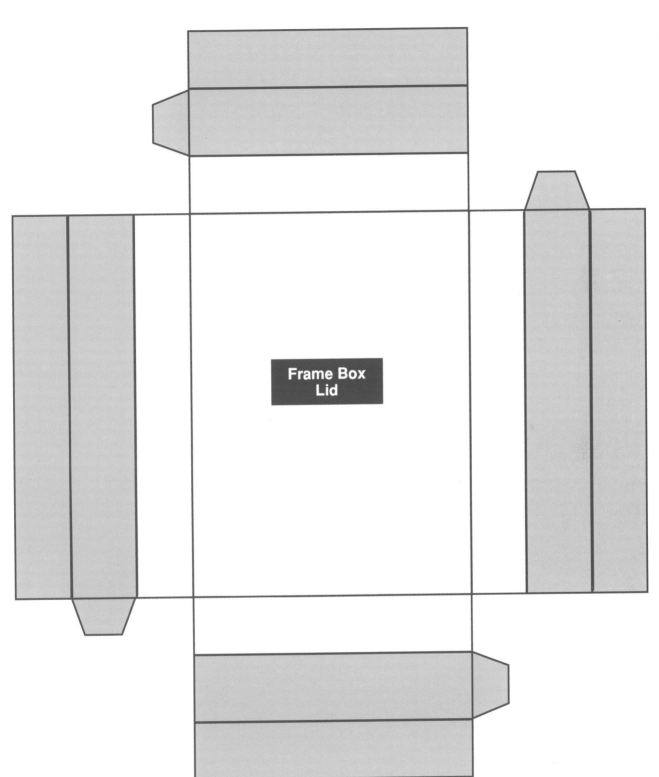

**Frame Box
Lid**

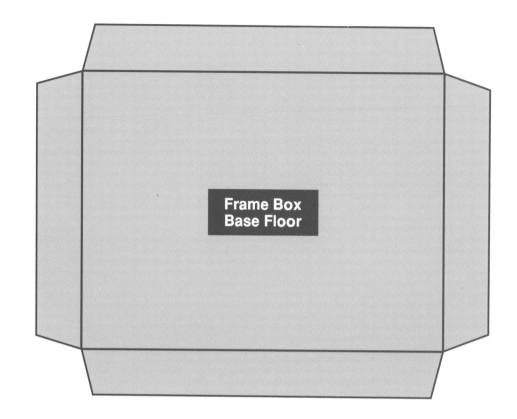

**Frame Box
Base Floor**

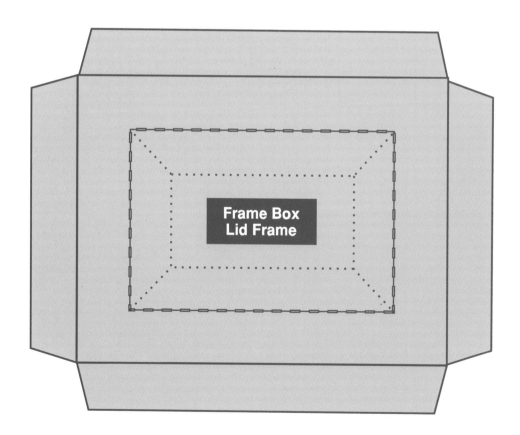

**Frame Box
Lid Frame**

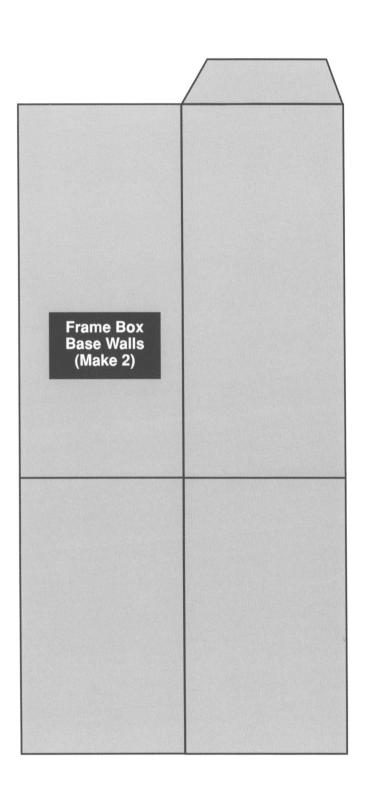

**Frame Box
Base Walls
(Make 2)**

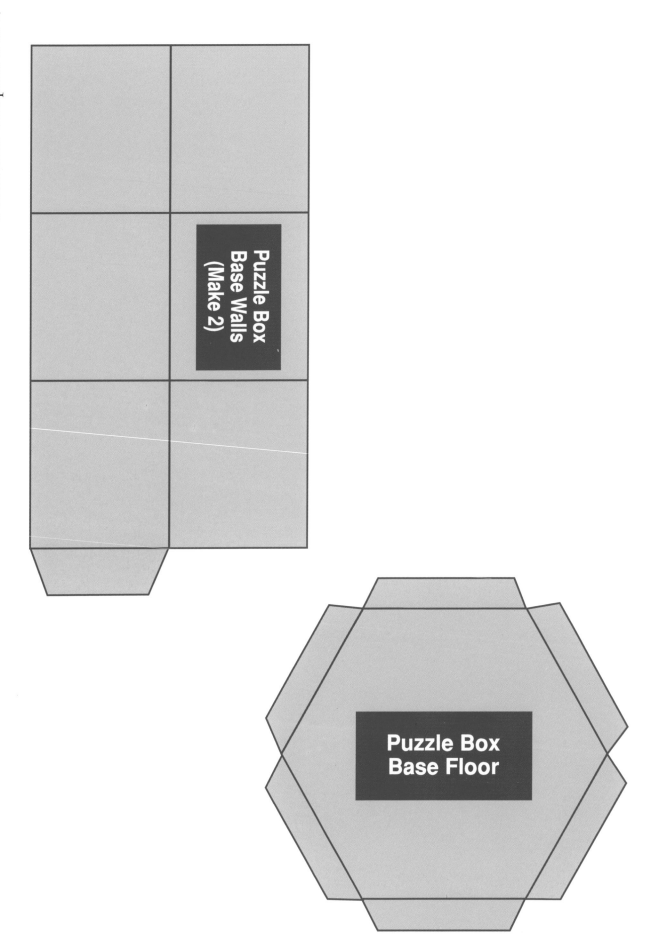

Puzzle Box
Base Walls
(Make 2)

**Puzzle Box
Base Floor**

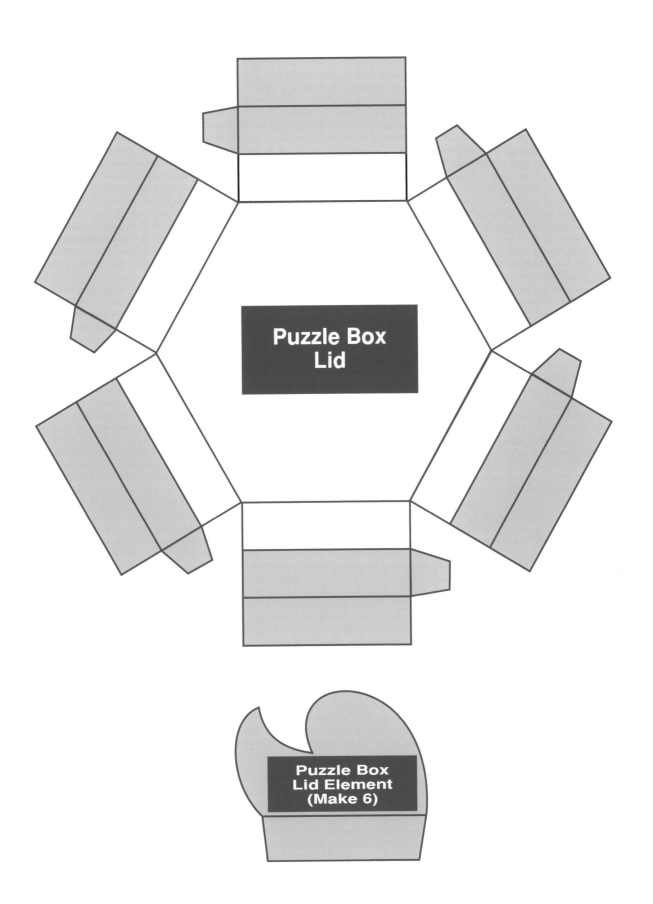

**Puzzle Box
Lid**

**Puzzle Box
Lid Element
(Make 6)**

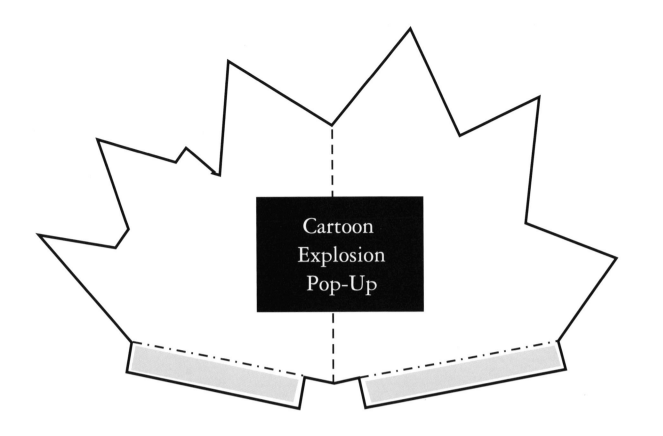

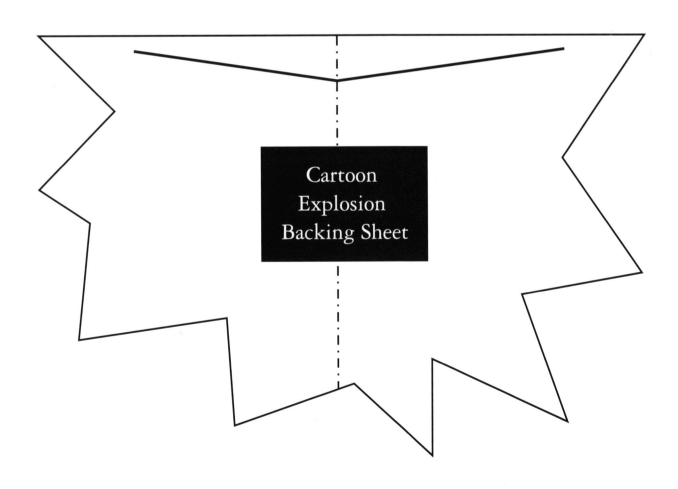

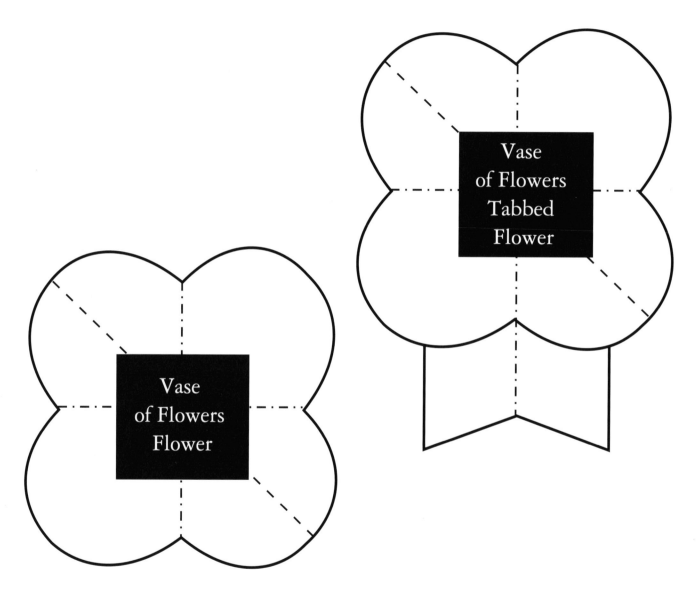

Vase
of Flowers
Flower

Vase
of Flowers
Tabbed
Flower

Guitar

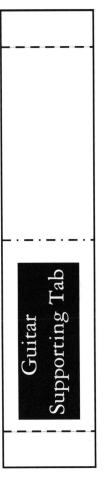

Guitar Supporting Tab

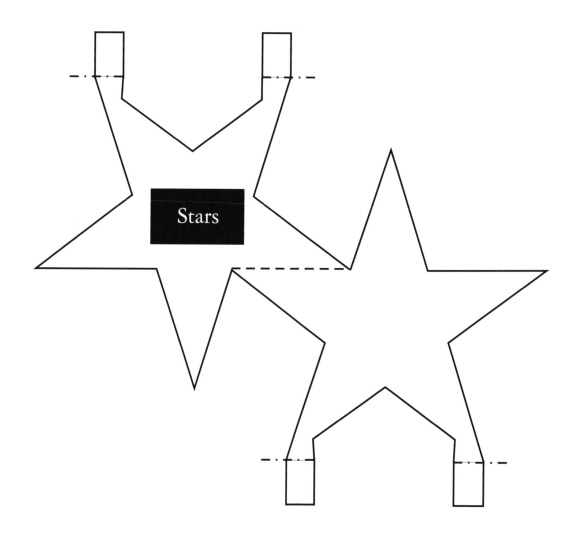

Stars

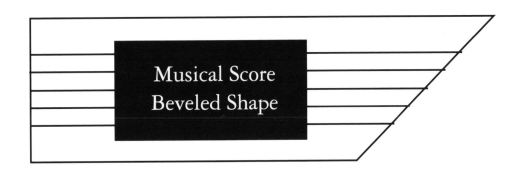

Musical Score
Rectangular Shape

Musical Score
Beveled Shape

Celebration
Wine Bottle

VIN

Wine Glass

Celebration Large Strap

Celebration Small Strap

LOTUS PETALS

LOTUS CENTER

LILY PAD

Posy Template

POSY
DAISY

POSY
CUP

SULPHUR
BUTTERFLY

POSY STEM

SWALLOWTAIL
BUTTERFLY

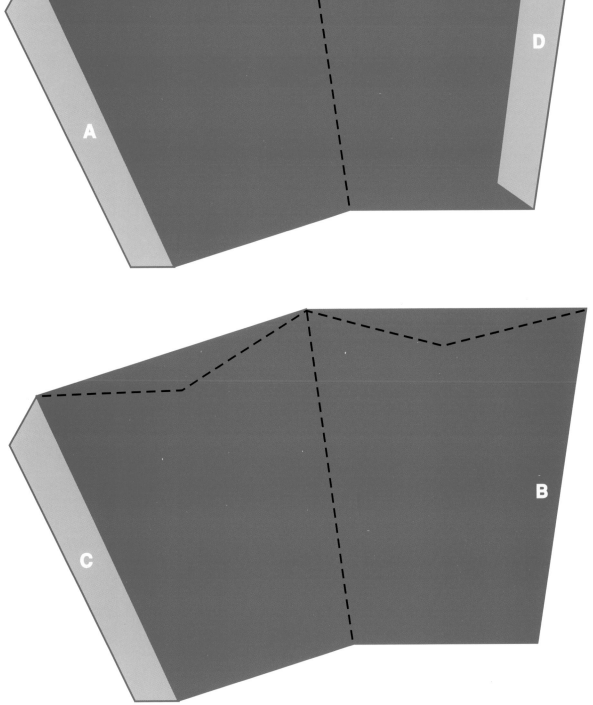

Vase Template

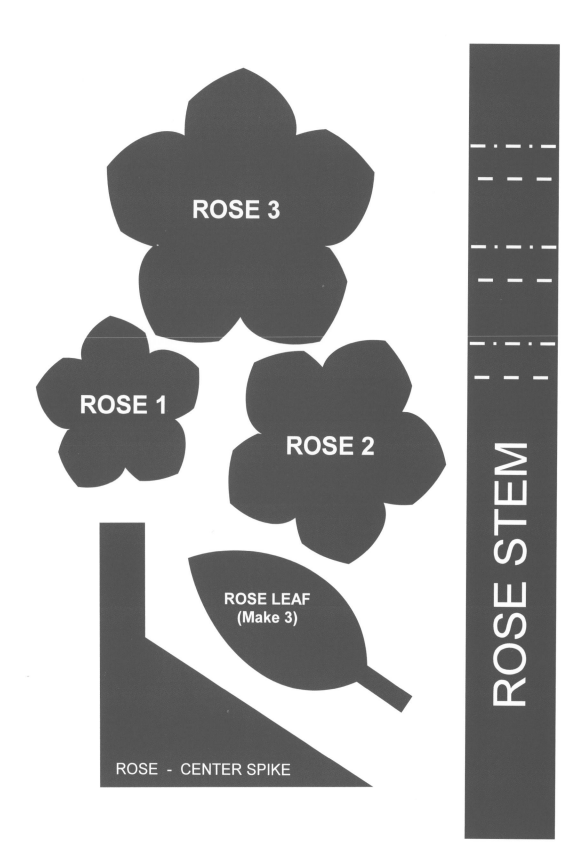

ROSE 3

ROSE 1

ROSE 2

ROSE LEAF
(Make 3)

ROSE - CENTER SPIKE

ROSE STEM